Cybersecurity for Developers

Master OWASP Essentials and Secure Web Apps with HTTP Security Headers

Gabriel Stones

Copyright

Table of Contents

Part 1:

Foundations of Web Application Security for Developers

Chapter 1

The Developer's Role in Cybersecurity: Shifting Left

If you're picking up this book, you're likely someone who builds things – you're a developer, a creator in the digital world. And if you're like me, you probably got into coding because you love to solve problems, to bring ideas to life with lines of text that magically transform into interactive experiences.

But in today's world, building amazing things isn't enough. We also have a crucial responsibility to build secure things. Think of it like this: you wouldn't build a house with faulty wiring or a shaky foundation, no matter how beautiful it looked, right? The same principle applies to the software we create.

For too long, security has often been seen as something that happens after the fact. We write our code, we deploy our applications, and then maybe a security team comes in to poke holes and tell us what we did wrong. That approach, while well-intentioned, is like trying to add armor to a car after it's already been in a crash. It's reactive, often costly, and doesn't always address the root of the problem.

That's where the idea of "Shifting Left" comes in. It's a fundamental change in how we think about security, urging us to move security considerations earlier in the software development lifecycle – closer to the "left" side of the timeline, towards the initial stages of planning and coding.

Understanding the Shared Responsibility Model: We're All in This Together

Before we dive deeper into "Shifting Left," we need to understand a core principle that underpins it: the Shared Responsibility Model. In the world of web security, especially with the rise of cloud computing and complex application architectures, security isn't just one person's or one team's job. It's a collaborative effort.

Imagine you're renting an apartment. The landlord is responsible for the structural integrity of the building, the security of the main entrances, and maybe even the plumbing and electrical systems up to a certain point. But you, the tenant, are responsible for the security of your own belongings inside the apartment, for locking your doors, and for using the utilities responsibly.

The same goes for web security:

Cloud Providers (like AWS, Azure, Google Cloud): They take responsibility for the security of the cloud infrastructure itself – the physical data centers, the network infrastructure, and the core services they offer. They ensure their platforms are resilient and protected.

Security Teams within Your Organization: They play a vital role in setting security policies, conducting penetration testing, monitoring for threats, and providing guidance and tools to development teams.

And here's the crucial part for us, the developers: We are responsible for the security in the cloud and in our applications. This includes the code we write, how we handle data, how we configure our applications, and the security implications of the libraries and frameworks we use.

We can't simply assume that because we're deploying to a "secure" cloud platform or have a dedicated security team, our applications will automatically be safe. The vulnerabilities that attackers exploit often reside within the application logic we create. If we write insecure code, mishandle user input, or misconfigure our systems, we create openings for malicious actors, no matter how secure the underlying infrastructure might be.

Think of it like building a beautiful website on a rock-solid server. If your website code has gaping security holes, it's like leaving the front door of that sturdy building wide open. The strength of the foundation won't matter much then.

Why Security Should Be a Core Part of the Development Lifecycle: Baking Security In, Not Just Sprinkling It On Top

This brings us directly to why "Shifting Left" is so important. For too long, security has been treated like an afterthought, something to be bolted on at the end of the development process. We'd build our features, get them working, and then maybe run a security scan or have a penetration test done.

But imagine trying to fix a structural flaw in a skyscraper after it's already been built. It's incredibly difficult, time-consuming, and expensive. It's much more efficient and effective to design the skyscraper with structural integrity in mind from the very beginning.

The same logic applies to our software. By integrating security considerations early in the Software Development Lifecycle (SDLC) – by "shifting left" – we can:

* Catch vulnerabilities early: Identifying and fixing security flaws during the design or development phases is significantly cheaper and less disruptive than dealing with them in production. A small code change early on is far less painful than a major security patch after a breach.

* Build more secure applications by default: When security is a core consideration from the

outset, it influences our architectural decisions, our coding practices, and the technologies we choose. We start thinking about potential threats and how to mitigate them as we're building, not as an afterthought.

* Reduce the burden on security teams: By proactively addressing common vulnerabilities in our code, we free up our security teams to focus on more complex threats, strategic initiatives, and providing us with better guidance and tools. It becomes a more collaborative and less reactive relationship.

* Improve the overall quality and reliability of our software: Secure software is often more robust and less prone to unexpected failures. Security and quality go hand-in-hand.

* Save time and money in the long run: Fixing security issues late in the development cycle or after a breach can be incredibly costly in terms of developer time, incident response, legal fees, and damage to reputation. Investing in security early is a smart long-term strategy.

Common Security Misconceptions Among Developers: Let's Clear the Air

Now, let's be honest. Sometimes, as developers, we might have certain assumptions or beliefs about security that aren't entirely accurate. These misconceptions can hinder our ability to embrace the "Shift Left" approach. Let's address some of the common ones:

"Security is someone else's job." We've already touched on this with the Shared Responsibility Model, but it's worth reiterating. While security teams are crucial, they can't be everywhere all the time. The code we write is a primary attack vector, and we have a direct responsibility to ensure it's as secure as possible.

"My application isn't important enough to be a target." This is a dangerous mindset. Attackers often use automated tools to scan for vulnerabilities across a wide range of applications, regardless of their size or perceived importance. Your application might be a stepping stone to a larger target, a source of valuable data you might not even realize you have, or simply an easy target for opportunistic attackers.

"As long as I use a secure framework, I'm safe." Modern frameworks often come with built-in security features, which is fantastic. However, these features are only effective if we use them correctly. Misconfiguring a secure framework or ignoring its security best practices can still leave our applications vulnerable. Think of it like having a car with airbags – they'll only protect you if you wear your seatbelt and drive safely.

"Security testing at the end is sufficient." Waiting until the very end of the development process to test for security vulnerabilities is like waiting until the end of a marathon to start training. You might identify problems, but fixing them at that stage can be incredibly difficult and require significant rework. Integrating security testing throughout the development process is much more effective.

"Security is too complex and slows down development." While the world of cybersecurity is vast and constantly evolving, the fundamental principles and common vulnerabilities are understandable and manageable. By integrating security early, we can often avoid major security overhauls later, which can actually speed up the overall development process in the long run. It's about building security in, not tacking it on.

"My code is unique, so it's inherently secure." Security through obscurity is not real security. Attackers often target common coding patterns and known vulnerabilities. Just because your code is different doesn't mean it's immune to attack. In fact, unique or less common code might even have undiscovered vulnerabilities.

By recognizing and challenging these misconceptions, we can start to cultivate a more security-aware mindset in our daily development practices.

The Cost of Neglecting Security: Real-World Wake-Up Calls

The consequences of neglecting security in our applications can be severe, impacting not just businesses but also the lives of individuals who use our software. Let's look at some real-world examples that should serve as stark reminders of why security needs to be a top priority:

* Massive Data Breaches: We've all heard the headlines – companies losing millions of users' personal data, including sensitive information like credit card numbers, social security numbers, and passwords. These breaches can lead to significant financial losses for the affected organizations (fines, legal battles, reputational damage, loss of customer trust) and devastating consequences for individuals (identity theft, financial fraud). Developers play a critical role in preventing these breaches by implementing secure data handling, storage, and transmission practices.

 * Website Defacements and Downtime: Imagine a popular website suddenly displaying offensive messages or becoming completely unavailable. This can severely damage a company's reputation, disrupt business operations, and lead to significant financial losses. Vulnerabilities in web application code and infrastructure can be exploited to deface websites or launch Denial of Service (DoS) attacks. Secure coding practices and proper server configuration are essential to prevent these incidents.

* Financial Fraud and Theft: Applications that handle financial transactions are prime targets for attackers. Vulnerabilities in these systems can be exploited to carry out unauthorized transactions, steal financial data, or manipulate account balances. Developers working on e-commerce platforms, banking applications, or any system that deals with money have an immense responsibility to ensure the security of these critical functions.

* Supply Chain Attacks: In today's interconnected world, attackers are increasingly targeting the software supply chain. By compromising third-party libraries, dependencies, or tools that developers use, attackers can gain access to a wide range of applications. Developers need to be aware of the risks associated with external dependencies and implement robust dependency management practices, including regular security checks and updates.

* Reputational Damage and Loss of Customer Trust: In the digital age, trust is paramount. A security breach can erode customer trust in an

instant, and once lost, it's incredibly difficult to regain. Users are increasingly aware of security risks and are more likely to abandon applications and services that have a history of security incidents. Building secure applications demonstrates a commitment to protecting user data and fosters long-term trust.

These are just a few examples, and the threat landscape is constantly evolving. As developers, we are often the first line of defense against these attacks. Understanding the potential costs of neglecting security should be a powerful motivator to make it a core part of our development process.

Adopting a Security-First Mindset: Principles and Practices for Building Secure Software

So, how do we actually adopt this "Security-First" mindset? It's not just about knowing the theory; it's about integrating security considerations into our daily development practices. Here are some key principles and practices we can embrace:

 * Assume Everything Can Be Malicious: This is a fundamental principle of secure development.

Never trust user input or data from external sources. Always validate and sanitize all input before processing it to prevent injection attacks and other vulnerabilities. Treat every piece of external data as potentially harmful until proven otherwise.

* Principle of Least Privilege: Grant only the necessary permissions to users, processes, and systems. This limits the potential damage if a component is compromised. For example, a user should only have access to the features they need to perform their job, and a process should only have the permissions required for its specific tasks.

* Defense in Depth: Implement multiple layers of security controls. Think of it like having multiple locks on your door. If one layer fails, others are in place to provide protection. This could include input validation, firewalls, encryption, secure coding practices, and more.

* Keep it Simple (KISS Principle): Complex systems are often harder to understand, test, and secure. Strive for simplicity in your design and implementation. The more complex your code,

the higher the chance of introducing subtle vulnerabilities.

* Stay Updated: The world of cybersecurity is constantly changing. New threats and vulnerabilities are discovered regularly. We need to commit to continuous learning, staying informed about the latest security trends, best practices, and vulnerabilities in the technologies we use. Follow security blogs, attend webinars, and engage with the security community.

* Code Reviews with Security in Mind: Make security a first-class citizen in your code review process. Train developers to identify common security vulnerabilities in code and encourage discussions about potential security implications during reviews.

* Automate Security Testing: Integrate security testing tools (like static analysis, dynamic analysis, and software composition analysis) into your Continuous Integration/Continuous Deployment (CI/CD) pipelines. This allows you to automatically identify vulnerabilities early and often in the development process.

* Foster a Culture of Security: Encourage open communication about security within your team and organization. Make it a shared responsibility and celebrate security successes. Create an environment where developers feel comfortable raising security concerns and learning from each other.

* Embrace Threat Modeling: Proactively think about potential threats to your application and design security controls to mitigate those risks. This involves understanding your application's architecture, identifying potential attack vectors, and determining the likelihood and impact of those threats.

Introduction to Threat Modeling for Developers: Thinking Like the Bad Guys (So You Can Stop Them)

Finally, let's introduce a powerful practice that embodies the "Shift Left" philosophy: Threat Modeling. Essentially, threat modeling is a structured way of identifying, evaluating, and mitigating potential security threats to your application.

As developers, we have a unique perspective on how our applications are built and how they function. This makes us invaluable in the threat modeling process. We need to start thinking like an attacker – how could someone try to exploit our system? What are the potential weaknesses? What valuable assets are we trying to protect?

Here's a basic overview of the threat modeling process that developers can actively participate in:

* Understand the System: Before you can identify threats, you need to have a clear understanding of your application's architecture, its different components, how data flows through it, and how it interacts with other systems. Creating diagrams and documenting these aspects is crucial.

* Identify Potential Threats: This is where you put on your "attacker hat." Brainstorm potential threats to each component and interaction you've identified. Think about common attack vectors like injection flaws, broken authentication, cross-site scripting, and more. Frameworks like STRIDE (Spoofing, Tampering, Repudiation,

Information Disclosure, Denial of Service, Elevation of Privilege) can be incredibly helpful in systematically categorizing and identifying potential threats.

* Analyze and Prioritize Threats: Once you have a list of potential threats, you need to evaluate their likelihood of occurring and the potential impact if they were to be exploited. Focus on the threats that pose the greatest risk to your application and its users. This prioritization will help you focus your mitigation efforts effectively.

* Develop Mitigation Strategies: For each prioritized threat, you need to define security controls and countermeasures that can be implemented to prevent or reduce the impact of the attack. This might involve changes to your code, your application's design, the infrastructure it runs on, or the way you handle data.

* Document and Review: It's essential to document your threat model, the identified threats, your analysis, and the mitigation strategies you've put in place. Threat modeling is

not a one-time activity; it should be a living document that is regularly reviewed and updated as your application evolves and new threats emerge.

By actively participating in threat modeling, we as developers can proactively identify potential security weaknesses in our applications early in the development process. This allows us to design and build more secure systems from the outset, rather than trying to patch vulnerabilities later on.

Wrapping Up Chapter 1: Embracing the Shift

This first chapter has been all about setting the stage. We've explored the critical concept of "Shifting Left" and why it's essential for modern web development. We've understood the Shared Responsibility Model, debunked common misconceptions about security, and examined the real-world costs of neglecting it. We've also introduced key principles for adopting a security-first mindset and touched upon the powerful practice of threat modeling.

As we move forward in this book, we'll delve into the specifics of OWASP essentials and how to implement robust security measures like HTTP security headers. But remember, the fundamental shift in mindset we've discussed here – taking ownership of security, thinking proactively, and integrating security into every stage of development – will be the foundation for building truly secure and resilient web applications.

Let's embrace the "Shift Left" together and make security an integral part of how we create the digital world. The responsibility, and the power to make a difference, lies with us, the developers.

Chapter 2:

Core Web Application Vulnerabilities: An Introduction to OWASP

In the ever-evolving landscape of web development, crafting elegant and functional applications is only half the battle. The other, equally critical aspect is ensuring these digital creations are robust and resilient against a myriad of threats lurking in the online world. As developers, we are not just builders; we are also, by necessity, the first line of defense for the applications we create and the users who rely on them.

This chapter serves as our initial foray into the crucial domain of web application security. We will explore the fundamental weaknesses that can make our applications susceptible to attacks. To effectively navigate this complex terrain, we will turn to the invaluable guidance of the Open Web Application Security Project, more commonly known as OWASP.

Understanding OWASP: Your Ally in Web Security

Think of OWASP as a global, open-source community driven by a shared mission: to make software more secure. It's a collaborative effort of security experts, developers, academics, and enthusiasts who pool their knowledge and experience to identify, document, and address the most prevalent web application security risks.

For developers, OWASP is an indispensable resource. It provides a wealth of freely available materials, including methodologies, tools, documentation, and perhaps most notably, the OWASP Top Ten. This regularly updated list represents a broad consensus on the ten most critical web application security risks. It's not just a list; it's a powerful awareness document that highlights the vulnerabilities developers need to understand and address proactively.

By familiarizing ourselves with OWASP and its resources, we gain access to a constantly evolving body of knowledge that reflects the current threat landscape. It empowers us to move beyond simply reacting to security incidents and instead build security into the very fabric of our applications.

The Landscape of Web Application Vulnerabilities: A Developer's Perspective

Web applications, by their very nature, involve interactions between users, servers, and databases. This intricate dance of data exchange creates numerous potential points of weakness that malicious actors can exploit. Understanding these common vulnerabilities is the first crucial step in writing secure code.

While the OWASP Top Ten provides a focused view of the most critical risks, it's important to recognize that the world of web security is broader. However, the Top Ten serves as an excellent starting point for developers to grasp the fundamental categories of vulnerabilities they will encounter and must learn to defend against.

Over the course of this book, we will delve deeply into each of these categories, exploring not just what they are, but more importantly, how they manifest in the code we write and the configurations we manage. We will equip you with practical knowledge and techniques to prevent these vulnerabilities from creeping into your applications.

For now, let's take a high-level look at some of the core vulnerability categories that OWASP and the broader security community emphasize. Think of these as the major fault lines that can compromise the integrity, confidentiality, and availability of your web applications:

Injection: Imagine an attacker cleverly inserting malicious commands or data into input fields that your application then unknowingly executes. This could lead to unauthorized access to your database (SQL Injection), the execution of arbitrary system commands (Command Injection), or other harmful actions. As developers, we must learn to treat all user input with suspicion and sanitize it rigorously.

Broken Authentication: This category revolves around flaws in how your application verifies the identity of users and manages their sessions. Weak password policies, insecure session handling, or allowing brute-force attacks can all lead to unauthorized access to user accounts and sensitive data. Robust authentication and session management are paramount for protecting user identities.

Cross-Site Scripting (XSS): Consider a scenario where an attacker injects malicious scripts into your web application that are then executed in the browsers of other users. This can allow the attacker to steal session cookies, redirect users to malicious sites, or even deface your website. Developers must understand how to properly handle user-generated content and encode output to prevent XSS attacks.

Insecure Design: This relatively new category in the OWASP Top Ten highlights fundamental flaws in the architecture and design of an application that make it inherently vulnerable.

Security should not be an afterthought; it needs to be baked into the design from the very beginning.

Security Misconfiguration: Sometimes, vulnerabilities arise not from flaws in the code itself, but from incorrect or insecure configurations of the web server, application server, databases, or other components. Developers and system administrators must work together to ensure all parts of the application ecosystem are securely configured.

Vulnerable and Outdated Components: Just like any software, the libraries and frameworks we use in our web applications can have known security vulnerabilities. Failing to keep these components up-to-date with the latest security patches can expose our applications to significant risks. Dependency management is a crucial skill for developers.

Identification and Authentication Failures: This category focuses on issues related to how users are identified and how their identity is verified. Weaknesses here can lead to account takeover and other unauthorized actions.

Software and Data Integrity Failures: This encompasses vulnerabilities related to assumptions about software updates, critical data, and CI/CD pipelines without proper integrity verification. Attackers might be able to compromise these systems and inject malicious code or data.

Security Logging and Monitoring Failures: If security-relevant events are not adequately logged and monitored, it becomes incredibly difficult to detect, respond to, and recover from security incidents. Developers need to implement robust logging and monitoring mechanisms.

Server-Side Request Forgery (SSRF): Imagine an attacker tricking your server into making requests to unintended internal or external resources. This can lead to the exposure of sensitive internal data or allow the attacker to interact with other systems behind your firewall.

Setting the Stage for Secure Development

This overview provides a glimpse into the common pitfalls that can plague web applications. As developers, understanding these vulnerabilities is not just an academic exercise; it's a fundamental requirement for building secure and reliable software.

In the chapters that follow, we will dissect each of these categories in detail. We will explore how these vulnerabilities are exploited, examine code examples that illustrate common mistakes, and, most importantly, equip you with the knowledge and practical techniques to prevent them in your own projects.

By the end of this book, you will not only understand the OWASP Top Ten and the importance of HTTP security headers, but you will also have the skills and mindset to build web applications that are resilient against these core vulnerabilities. Let's continue our journey into the world of secure web development.

Chapter 3:

Diving Deep: Mastering HTTP Fundamentals for Web Security

Alright folks, let's talk about the unsung hero of the web: HTTP. You interact with it every single day, whether you're browsing your favorite sites, using web apps, or even when your mobile apps pull data from the internet. It's the language that your browser and web servers use to communicate. And just like understanding the grammar and nuances of any language is crucial for clear communication, a solid grasp of HTTP is absolutely essential for building secure web applications.

Think of HTTP as the foundation upon which all our web creations stand. If that foundation has cracks or weaknesses, anything built on top of it is inherently vulnerable. In this chapter, we're going to roll up our sleeves and get intimately familiar with how HTTP works under the hood. We'll explore the structure of the messages exchanged, the different ways clients and servers talk to each other, and, most importantly, how this knowledge empowers us to write more secure code.

Peeking Under the Hood: Anatomy of HTTP Requests and Responses

At its heart, HTTP (Hypertext Transfer Protocol) is a simple yet powerful protocol. It's stateless, meaning each interaction between your browser (the client) and a web server is independent. Each time your browser asks for a webpage or sends data, it creates a brand new connection. This conversation happens through two key components: requests (what your browser sends) and responses (what the server sends back).

Let's dissect an HTTP request first. Imagine your browser asking a server for a specific webpage:

The Verb (or Method): This is like telling the server what you want to do with a particular

resource. Think of it as an action. Some common verbs you'll encounter are:

GET: "Hey server, I just want to get this information." This is used for retrieving data, like when you load a webpage. Ideally, GET requests shouldn't change anything on the server.

POST: "Server, I want to post this data to you, maybe to create a new account or submit a form." This is used for sending data to the server, often to create or update something.

PUT: "Server, I want to put this data here, replacing whatever was there before." Often used for updating an entire resource.

DELETE: "Server, please delete this resource." Used to remove something from the server.

HEAD: "Server, just give me the head of this information – the metadata, like when it was last modified, but not the actual content." Useful for checking things without downloading the whole thing.

OPTIONS: "Server, what options do you support for this resource? What verbs can I use?" This asks the server about the available methods.

Why should we care about the verb for security? Using the right verb is more than just good practice; it's a security consideration. For example, sensitive actions that change data (like placing an order or updating a profile) should never be done with a GET request where the data might end up in URLs, browser history, or server logs. These actions should use POST, PUT, or DELETE where the data is tucked away in the request body.

The Target (or Request-URI): This is like the address you're asking for – it identifies the specific resource on the server you want to interact with. It usually looks like a web address (URL) and points to a specific file or endpoint. Sometimes, it includes extra bits after a question mark (?), called query parameters, which are ways to send small pieces of data along with a GET request.

Security-wise: Be cautious about putting sensitive information directly in the URL via query parameters, especially with GET requests. These can be easily visible and logged in various places. Also, how we handle and interpret these

URIs on the server is critical to prevent attackers from trying to access resources they shouldn't (path traversal vulnerabilities).

The Version (HTTP/1.1, HTTP/2, HTTP/3): This tells the server which version of the HTTP protocol your browser is speaking. Newer versions like HTTP/2 and HTTP/3 bring performance improvements and different underlying mechanisms that can have subtle security implications to be aware of.

The Extra Information (Request Headers):

These are like extra instructions or context you send along with your request. They tell the server things like what kind of browser you're using (User-Agent), what types of data you can understand (Accept), any cookies the server previously sent you (Cookie), and sometimes even authentication details (Authorization).

Security spotlight on headers: Headers can contain sensitive stuff! Cookies often hold session IDs, and the Authorization header might contain tokens. We need to make sure these are protected in transit (using HTTPS) and that we're not accidentally exposing sensitive information through custom headers. Also, the server needs to be careful about blindly trusting all header information, as some can be manipulated by attackers.

The Payload (Request Body - Optional): For requests that send data to the server (like POST or PUT), the actual data is included in the message body. This could be the information you typed into a form, a JSON object for an API call, or even a file you're uploading.

Think secure input: Just like we discussed in the OWASP chapter, any data coming from the client in the request body is untrusted and needs rigorous validation and sanitization on the server to prevent all sorts of nasty attacks.

Now, let's flip the script and look at an HTTP response – what the server sends back to your browser:

The Status (Status Code and Reason Phrase): This is the server's way of telling your browser what happened with your request. The status code is a three-digit number that summarizes the outcome (e.g., 200 OK means everything went fine, 404 Not Found means the resource wasn't there). The reason phrase is a human-readable explanation of the code.

Security clues in status codes: Pay attention to these! A 401 Unauthorized tells you authentication is needed, while a 403 Forbidden means you're authenticated but don't have permission. Also, overly detailed error messages (like a 500 Internal Server Error revealing server internals) can be a security risk in production. We should aim for generic error messages for users while logging the specifics securely on the server. Redirects (3xx codes) also deserve our attention – we need to be careful about where we're redirecting users, especially if the redirect URL comes from user input.

The Version (Same as the request, usually):
The HTTP version the server is using for its response.

The Extra Information (Response Headers):
Just like requests have headers, responses do too. These provide extra context about the response, like the type of content being sent

(Content-Type), its size (Content-Length), instructions for setting cookies on your browser (Set-Cookie), and information about the server itself (Server).

Security-critical response headers: This is where the magic of HTTP Security Headers happens! These special headers tell your browser how to behave to enhance security. We're talking about things like Content-Security-Policy (to prevent XSS), Strict-Transport-Security (to enforce HTTPS), X-Content-Type-Options (to prevent MIME sniffing), and X-Frame-Options (to prevent clickjacking). We'll be diving deep into these later, but for now, know that these headers are like security instructions we give directly to the browser. Also, be mindful of the Server header – revealing the exact server software and version can give attackers a head start in finding known vulnerabilities. It's often a good idea to suppress this in production.

* The Payload (Response Body - Optional): This is the actual content the server is sending back – the HTML of a webpage, the JSON data for an API, an image, a video, etc.

Secure content delivery: If the response body contains sensitive information, it absolutely must be transmitted over a secure connection (HTTPS). Also, if the server is dynamically generating content that includes user input, we need to be meticulous about encoding it properly to prevent XSS vulnerabilities.

Choosing Your Weapon Wisely: Understanding HTTP Methods and Security

The HTTP method you choose for an action isn't just a matter of semantics; it has real security implications. Think of it like using the right tool for the job:

GET is for Looking, Not Touching: Use GET solely for retrieving data. It should be idempotent (doing it multiple times has the same result) and safe (it shouldn't have any side effects on the server, like modifying data). Never use GET to perform actions that change the state of your application or handle sensitive data in the URL.

POST is for Sending and Creating: Use POST to send data to the server, often to create new resources or perform actions that have side effects. The data is usually in the request body, which is generally safer than putting it in the URL.

PUT and PATCH are for Updating: Use PUT to replace an entire resource and PATCH to partially update it. These methods require careful authorization to ensure only the right users can modify data.

DELETE is for Removing: Use DELETE to remove a resource. Like PUT and PATCH, proper authorization is crucial.

Be Mindful of Others: Methods like HEAD, OPTIONS, and especially TRACE have their uses, but also potential security risks. For instance, TRACE can sometimes be exploited to reveal internal headers, so it's often disabled on production servers.

The Golden Rule: Always pick the HTTP method that accurately reflects the action you intend to perform. Enforce strict authorization checks on all methods that modify data.

Status Updates with Security Context: What the Server's Telling You Matters

HTTP status codes are more than just error messages; they provide crucial context about the outcome of a request, and this context can have security implications:

401 Unauthorized vs. 403 Forbidden: Knowing the difference helps you implement proper authentication (verifying who the user is) and authorization (verifying what they're allowed to do). A 401 means they need to log in, while a 403 means they're logged in but don't have permission for that specific resource.

Being Vague Can Be Safer (Sometimes with 404): While it's tempting to be very specific with "Not Found" errors, sometimes a generic "Not Found" can prevent attackers from easily discovering which resources actually exist on your server.

Don't Spill the Beans with 500 Errors: Detailed server error messages in production environments can reveal sensitive information about your server setup and potential weaknesses. Log the specifics securely on the server but provide a generic error message to the client.

Watch Out for Redirects (3xx): Be extremely cautious about redirects, especially if the target URL is based on user input. Attackers can exploit this for phishing scams. Always validate and sanitize redirect URLs server-side.

Security Tip: Use HTTP status codes accurately to provide meaningful feedback. Be mindful of the level of detail you expose in error messages. Treat redirects with caution.

The Sticky Situation: Cookies and Sessions in a Stateless World

HTTP is stateless, but most web applications need to maintain some form of state, like remembering who's logged in or what's in a user's shopping cart. This is where cookies and sessions come into play. Understanding how they work and how to secure them is paramount.

Cookies: Small but Significant: Cookies are tiny pieces of data that a server can ask your browser to store. Your browser then sends these cookies back to the server with subsequent requests to the same website. They're used for everything from remembering your preferences to tracking your activity.

Security must-haves for cookies:

Secure Flag: Make sure to set the Secure flag so that the cookie is only transmitted over HTTPS, preventing eavesdropping on unencrypted connections.

HttpOnly Flag: This crucial flag prevents JavaScript on the page from accessing the cookie, significantly reducing the risk of session hijacking via Cross-Site Scripting (XSS) attacks.

SameSite Attribute: This helps protect against Cross-Site Request Forgery (CSRF) attacks by controlling when the browser sends the cookie along with cross-origin requests. Set it to Strict or Lax based on your application's needs.

Expiration: Set appropriate expiration times for your cookies. Persistent cookies should have well-defined lifespans.

Scope (Domain and Path): Limit the domains and paths for which the cookie is valid to minimize its exposure.

Sessions: Remembering You on the Server: Sessions provide a way to maintain user state on the server. When you log in, the server creates a unique session for you and gives your browser a session identifier (usually stored in a cookie). For all subsequent requests from you, your browser sends this ID back, allowing the server to remember your logged-in state and associated data.

Key security for sessions:

Strong Session IDs: Generate session IDs that are cryptographically random and unpredictable.

Secure Transmission: Just like cookies, session IDs (usually in cookies) need the Secure and HttpOnly flags.

Session Timeout: Implement reasonable session timeouts. Idle sessions should expire after a period of inactivity.

Session Regeneration: After a successful login, regenerate the session ID to prevent session fixation attacks.

Secure Storage: Store session data securely on the server, not in easily accessible locations.

Defense Against Hijacking: Implement mechanisms to detect and prevent session hijacking attempts (e.g., tracking IP addresses or user agents, though these can have drawbacks).

The Unsung Heroes: Introduction to HTTP Security Headers

Finally, let's touch on something incredibly powerful for web security: HTTP Security Headers. These are special instructions that your server sends to the browser in the HTTP response. They tell the browser how to behave to protect your users and your application from various attacks. Think of them as adding extra layers of security without necessarily changing your core application code.

We'll dedicate a whole section to these later, but here's a quick peek at their significance:

Content-Security-Policy (CSP): Your ultimate weapon against XSS. It lets you define trusted sources for various types of content (scripts, styles, images, etc.), and the browser will block anything from untrusted sources.

Strict-Transport-Security (HSTS): Forces the browser to always use HTTPS for your site, even if a user types http:// or clicks an old link. This is crucial for preventing Man-in-the-Middle attacks.

X-Content-Type-Options: nosniff: Prevents the browser from trying to guess the content type of a response (MIME sniffing), which can be exploited in some attacks.

X-Frame-Options / Content-Security-Policy frame-ancestors: Helps prevent clickjacking by controlling whether your site can be embedded in <frame>, <iframe>, or <object> elements on other websites.

Referrer-Policy: Controls how much information about the previous page is sent in the Referer header when a user navigates away from your site, helping with privacy and preventing some information leaks.

And More! There are other powerful headers like Permissions-Policy (controlling browser features), Expect-CT (for Certificate Transparency), and others that add valuable security layers.

Why are these headers so important? They're a proactive way to tell the browser, "Hey, here are the security rules I want you to enforce for this website." By setting them correctly, you can significantly reduce the attack surface of your application and provide a much safer experience for your users.

Wrapping Up: HTTP is Your Friend (When You Understand It)

Mastering HTTP fundamentals isn't just about knowing the technical details of how the web works; it's about understanding the underlying mechanisms that can be exploited if we're not careful. By diving deep into the structure of requests and responses, understanding the implications of HTTP methods and status codes, and appreciating the role of cookies and sessions, we arm ourselves with the knowledge to build more secure web applications. And by embracing the power of HTTP Security Headers, we can add another vital layer of defense.

As we move forward, this understanding of HTTP will be crucial as we delve into specific OWASP vulnerabilities and learn how to leverage these fundamentals to protect our applications. So, keep this knowledge in your toolkit – it's one of the most important tools you have as a web developer who cares about security.

Part 2:

OWASP Top Ten in Depth: Prevention and Mitigation for Developers

Chapter 4:

Injection Attacks: SQL, NoSQL, and Command Injection.

In this chapter, we're going to dissect the world of injection attacks, looking at the common types that developers need to be acutely aware of: SQL Injection, NoSQL Injection, and Command Injection. We'll understand how these flaws creep into our code, how malicious actors exploit them, and, most importantly, the concrete steps we can take to prevent them from ever happening in our applications.

Understanding Different Types of Injection Vulnerabilities: When Trusting Input Goes Wrong

At its core, an injection attack occurs when an attacker is able to insert malicious code or data into an application's input fields, and that input is then processed in an unintended way by the backend system. Think of it like a Trojan Horse – seemingly harmless input that carries a hidden, malicious payload.

There are several types of injection attacks, but the most common and impactful ones we'll focus on are:

SQL Injection (SQLi): This type of attack targets applications that use SQL databases. By injecting malicious SQL code into input fields (like login forms, search boxes, or URL parameters), an attacker can manipulate the database queries being executed. This can lead to a wide range of consequences, from data breaches and data corruption to bypassing authentication and even executing arbitrary commands on the database server.

NoSQL Injection: With the rise of NoSQL databases (like MongoDB, Couchbase, Cassandra), a new class of injection vulnerabilities has emerged. While the syntax and structure differ from SQL, the underlying principle is the same: injecting malicious queries or commands into the NoSQL database query language to gain unauthorized access or manipulate data.

Command Injection (OS Command Injection): This vulnerability arises when an application executes operating system commands based on user-supplied input without proper sanitization. An attacker can inject malicious commands that will be executed on the server's operating system, potentially leading to complete server compromise.

How Injection Flaws Occur in Developer Code: The Path of Untrusted Data
Injection vulnerabilities often stem from a fundamental mistake: trusting user-supplied input without proper validation and sanitization. When we, as developers, directly incorporate user input into database queries or system commands without cleaning it first, we open a door for attackers to manipulate that input for their malicious purposes.

Let's look at some simplified examples to illustrate how these flaws can appear in our code:

SQL Injection Example (in a hypothetical language):

```
string username = getInput("username");
string password = getInput("password");

string query = "SELECT * FROM users WHERE username = '" + username + "' AND password = '" + password + "'";

executeDatabaseQuery(query);
```

In this seemingly innocent code, if an attacker enters something like ' OR '1'='1 in the username field and any password in the password field, the resulting SQL query becomes:

```
SELECT * FROM users WHERE username = '' OR '1'='1' AND password = 'anypassword';
```

Since '1'='1' is always true, this modified query effectively bypasses the username and password check, potentially granting the attacker unauthorized access.

NoSQL Injection Example (MongoDB with JavaScript):

```
const username = req.body.username;
const password = req.body.password;

const query = { username: username, password: password };

db.collection('users').findOne(query).then(user => {
  // ... authentication logic ...
});
```

If an attacker provides a specially crafted username like {$gt: "}, depending on the specific NoSQL database and how it processes such operators, they might be able to bypass the username check. More complex NoSQL injection attacks can involve manipulating operators and query structures to extract or modify data.

Command Injection Example (in a hypothetical language):
string filename = getInput("filename");

string command = "convert image.jpg " + filename + ".png";

executeSystemCommand(command);

Here, if an attacker provides a filename like ; rm -rf /, the resulting command becomes:
convert image.jpg ; rm -rf /.png

The ; acts as a command separator, and the rm -rf / command (if executed with sufficient privileges) could wipe out the entire file system of the server.

The Common Thread: In all these examples, the vulnerability arises from directly using untrusted user input in a sensitive operation (database query or system command) without proper validation or escaping.

Preventing SQL Injection: Parameterized Queries and Prepared Statements to the Rescue

The most effective way to prevent SQL Injection attacks is to never directly embed user input into SQL queries. Instead, you should always use parameterized queries (also known as prepared statements).

Parameterized queries work by separating the SQL structure from the user-provided data. You define the SQL query with placeholders (parameters), and then you pass the user input as separate parameters to the database driver. The database driver then handles the proper escaping and quoting of the data, ensuring that it's treated as data, not as executable SQL code.

Example (Python with a database library like psycopg2 for PostgreSQL):

```
username = input("Enter username: ")
password = input("Enter password: ")

query = "SELECT * FROM users WHERE username = %s AND password = %s"
cursor.execute(query, (username, password))
user = cursor.fetchone()
```

In this example, %s are placeholders. The execute() method takes the query and a tuple of parameters. The database driver safely substitutes these parameters into the query, preventing any malicious SQL code in username or password from being executed.

Key Benefits of Parameterized Queries:
Complete Prevention of SQL Injection: By treating user input as data, they eliminate the possibility of attackers injecting malicious SQL code.

Improved Performance: Databases can often optimize prepared statements for repeated execution.

Cleaner Code: Separating SQL structure from data makes the code easier to read and maintain. This is a non-negotiable security practice for any application interacting with a SQL database.

Mitigating NoSQL Injection: Best Practices and ORM Considerations

Preventing NoSQL injection requires a similar mindset: treat all user input as untrusted. However, the specific techniques will vary depending on the NoSQL database you are using.

General Best Practices:

Input Validation: As with SQL, rigorously validate all user input to ensure it conforms to expected formats and lengths.

Avoid Dynamic Query Construction: Just like with SQL, try to avoid building NoSQL queries by concatenating strings with user input.

Use ORMs and Database Abstraction Layers Carefully: While Object-Document Mappers (ODMs) or database abstraction layers can help, they don't automatically guarantee protection against NoSQL injection. Ensure you understand how they handle user input in their query generation.

Be Aware of Database-Specific Operators: Understand the special operators and syntax of your NoSQL database and how they might be exploited. For example, in MongoDB, operators like $where, $expr, and certain query modifiers, if used with unsanitized user input, can lead to vulnerabilities.

Principle of Least Privilege: Ensure your database user accounts have only the necessary permissions. This limits the damage an attacker can do even if they manage to inject malicious queries.

Example (Node.js with Mongoose for MongoDB - illustrating a potential risk and a safer approach):

Potentially Vulnerable:

```
const { username } = req.body;
const query = { username: { $regex: '^' +
username + '$', $options: 'i' } };
User.findOne(query).then(user => { /* ... */ });
```

If an attacker crafts a malicious username containing special regex characters, they might be able to manipulate the query.

Safer Approach (using Mongoose's query building):

```
const { username } = req.body;
```

```
const query = { username: new RegExp('^' +
escapeRegex(username) + '$', 'i') }; // Using a
function to escape special regex characters
User.findOne(query).then(user => { /* ... */ });

function escapeRegex(text) {
    return   text.replace(/[-[\]{}()*+?.,\\^$|#\s]/g,
'\\$&');
}
```

While this example focuses on regex, the core
principle is to be aware of how user input
interacts with the database's query language and
to use safe methods for constructing queries.
Always consult the security documentation for
your specific NoSQL database.
Securing Against Command Injection: Input
Sanitization and Safe API Usage are Key
Command Injection vulnerabilities can be
particularly dangerous as they can lead to direct
control over the server's operating system. The
key to preventing them is to avoid executing
system commands based on user-provided input
whenever possible.

Best Practices:

Avoid System Calls: The most secure approach is to find alternative ways to achieve the desired functionality without resorting to executing external system commands. Many tasks can be accomplished using built-in language features or libraries.

Strict Input Sanitization: If you absolutely must execute system commands based on user input, implement extremely strict input validation and sanitization. Whitelist allowed characters and formats, and reject anything that doesn't conform. Be wary of metacharacters (like ;, |, &, $, `) that can be used to chain or redirect commands.

Use Safe APIs and Libraries: Many programming languages provide secure APIs for interacting with the operating system that abstract away the complexities and risks of directly executing shell commands. Use these whenever available. For example, instead of using system() or exec() to manipulate files, use the language's built-in file system libraries.

Principle of Least Privilege: Run your application with the minimum necessary privileges. If an attacker manages to inject a command, the damage they can do will be limited by the application's permissions.

Output Encoding: If you display the output of system commands in your application, make sure to properly encode it to prevent potential XSS if an attacker manages to inject malicious output.

Example (Illustrating a risky approach and a safer alternative in Python):

Risky:

```python
import os
filename = input("Enter filename: ")
command = f"ls -l {filename}"
os.system(command)
```

If a user enters ; cat /etc/passwd, this could potentially expose sensitive system information.

Safer (using the subprocess module):

```python
import subprocess
filename = input("Enter filename: ")
command = ["ls", "-l", filename]
```

```
try:
        result   =   subprocess.run(command,
capture_output=True, text=True, check=True)
    print(result.stdout)
except subprocess.CalledProcessError as e:
    print(f"Error: {e}")
```

The subprocess module, especially when using the list format for commands, helps to prevent shell interpretation of metacharacters in the input. The check=True argument also raises an exception if the command fails, which can be handled appropriately.

The Bottom Line: Treat All Input as Guilty Until Proven Innocent

The overarching principle to remember when dealing with injection vulnerabilities is to never trust user-supplied input directly. Always validate it to ensure it conforms to your expectations, and sanitize it to remove or escape any potentially malicious characters before using it in sensitive operations like database queries or system commands.

By adopting secure coding practices like using parameterized queries, being mindful of NoSQL-specific risks, and avoiding or carefully sanitizing input for system commands, we can effectively close the door on these prevalent and dangerous injection attacks. This proactive approach is a cornerstone of building secure web applications. In the next chapter, we'll move on to another critical area: Broken Authentication.

Chapter 5:

Broken Authentication: Secure User Management.

Think about it – if the very process of identifying and verifying who your users are is flawed, then all other security measures you put in place are built on shaky ground. It's like having a high-security vault with a flimsy lock on the front door.

In this chapter, we're going to thoroughly explore the common vulnerabilities that developers inadvertently introduce into authentication mechanisms. We'll look at everything from weak password policies to insecure session management and, most importantly, we'll equip you with the knowledge and practical techniques to build robust and secure user management systems that you can trust.

Common Authentication Vulnerabilities Developers Introduce: The Weak Links in the Chain

Authentication, at its core, is the process of verifying a user's identity. It answers the question, "Who are you?" When this process is broken or poorly implemented, it opens the door for attackers to impersonate legitimate users, gain unauthorized access to sensitive data, and wreak havoc. Here are some of the common pitfalls we, as developers, need to be hyper-aware of:

1) Weak Password Policies: This is often the first line of defense. If we allow users to choose easily guessable passwords (like "123456" or "password"), or if we don't enforce sufficient complexity requirements (minimum length, mix of characters), we're making it easy for attackers to crack accounts through brute-force attacks or dictionary attacks.

2) Insecure Password Storage: Even with strong passwords, if we store them insecurely on our servers, we're creating a massive target for attackers. Simply storing passwords in plain text or using weak or outdated hashing algorithms is a recipe for disaster in case of a data breach.

3) Vulnerable Login Mechanisms: Flaws in the login process itself can be exploited. This could include allowing unlimited login attempts (making brute-force attacks trivial), exposing error messages that reveal whether a username exists, or being susceptible to timing attacks that can help attackers guess credentials.

4) Insecure Session Management: Once a user is authenticated, their session needs to be managed securely. Vulnerabilities here can allow attackers to hijack a legitimate user's session and take over their account. Common issues include predictable session IDs, session fixation

vulnerabilities, and not properly invalidating sessions on logout.

5) Missing or Weak Multi-Factor Authentication (MFA): MFA adds an extra layer of security beyond just a username and password. If it's not implemented or if the implementation is weak, attackers who manage to obtain a user's password still have a much easier time gaining access.

6) Flaws in "Remember Me" Functionality: While convenient for users, "remember me" features need to be implemented carefully. If the tokens used to remember users are not stored and handled securely, they can be stolen and used to gain persistent unauthorized access.

7) Insecure Account Recovery Mechanisms: Password reset and account recovery features are essential but can also be a point of attack if not implemented securely. Weak security questions,

predictable reset links, or the ability to take over an account through these processes are serious vulnerabilities.

Implementing Strong Password Policies and Hashing Techniques: Building a Solid First Line of Defense

The foundation of secure authentication starts with strong passwords and storing them securely. Here's what we need to do:

Enforce Robust Password Policies: Don't leave password strength up to the user. Implement clear and strict policies:

Minimum Length: Enforce a reasonable minimum length (at least 12 characters is a good starting point).

Complexity Requirements: Require a mix of uppercase and lowercase letters, numbers, and special characters.

Password History: Prevent users from reusing recent passwords.

Regular Password Updates (Optional but Recommended): Encourage or even require users to change their passwords periodically.

Real-time Feedback: Provide users with feedback as they type their password to help them choose stronger ones.

Use Strong and Modern Hashing Algorithms: Never, ever store passwords in plain text. Instead, use a strong cryptographic hash function. A hash function takes an input (the password) and produces a fixed-size output (the hash) that is computationally infeasible to reverse. Modern and recommended algorithms include:

bcrypt: A widely respected and secure hashing algorithm that includes built-in salt and adaptive work factors (making it harder for attackers to use pre-computed tables or brute-force).

Argon2: A newer, memory-hard hashing algorithm that is also considered very secure and is a strong contender to bcrypt.

scrypt: Another memory-hard algorithm that is also a good choice.

Salt Your Hashes: A salt is a random, unique value that you generate for each password and store alongside its hash in the database. Salting prevents attackers from using pre-computed tables of common password hashes (rainbow tables) to crack passwords even if they manage to get ahold of your database. Each password should have its own unique, randomly generated salt.

Work Factor/Iteration Count: Algorithms like bcrypt and Argon2 allow you to adjust a "work factor" or "iteration count." This parameter controls how computationally expensive it is to hash a password. Increasing this makes it harder for attackers to brute-force hashes, but also increases the time it takes for legitimate users to log in. You need to find a balance that provides strong security without causing unacceptable delays.

Example (Python with the bcrypt library):

```python
import bcrypt

def hash_password(password):
    # Generate a random salt
    salt = bcrypt.gensalt()
    # Hash the password with the salt
```

```python
    hashed_password         =
bcrypt.hashpw(password.encode('utf-8'), salt)
        return   hashed_password.decode('utf-8'),
salt.decode('utf-8')

def   verify_password(stored_hash,   password,
salt):
    # Hash the provided password with the stored
salt
        hashed_attempt          =
bcrypt.hashpw(password.encode('utf-8'),
salt.encode('utf-8'))
    # Compare the generated hash with the stored
hash
        return   hashed_attempt.decode('utf-8')   ==
stored_hash

# Example usage:
password_to_hash = "mysecretpassword123"
hashed,              salt              =
hash_password(password_to_hash)
print(f"Hashed password: {hashed}")
print(f"Salt: {salt}")
```

```
provided_password = "mysecretpassword123"
if verify_password(hashed, provided_password,
salt):
    print("Password verified successfully!")
else:
    print("Password verification failed.")
```

Secure Session Management: Preventing Hijacking and Fixation

Once a user is successfully authenticated, we need to manage their session securely. A session represents a user's active interaction with our application over a period of time. Here's how to do it right:

Generate Strong and Random Session IDs: Session IDs should be unpredictable and cryptographically secure. Avoid using sequential or easily guessable IDs. Most modern frameworks provide mechanisms for generating secure session IDs.

Protect Session IDs in Transit: Always transmit session IDs (usually stored in cookies) over HTTPS. Set the Secure flag on session cookies to ensure they are only sent over encrypted connections.

Use the HttpOnly Flag: Set the HttpOnly flag on session cookies. This prevents client-side JavaScript from accessing the session ID, significantly mitigating the risk of session hijacking through XSS vulnerabilities.

Implement Session Timeouts: Sessions should have a limited lifespan. Implement both idle timeouts (inactivity-based) and absolute timeouts (based on the initial login time). This reduces the window of opportunity for attackers if a session ID is compromised.

Regenerate Session IDs After Login: After a user successfully authenticates, generate a new session ID for them. This helps prevent session fixation attacks, where an attacker might try to trick a user into using a session ID they already control.

Invalidate Sessions on Logout: When a user explicitly logs out, their session on the server should be completely invalidated, and the session cookie on the client should be cleared or expired.

Consider Additional Security Measures (Optional): For highly sensitive applications, you might consider additional measures like tying sessions to specific IP addresses or user agents. However, be aware that these can sometimes cause issues for legitimate users (e.g., if their IP address changes).

Multi-Factor Authentication (MFA) Implementation for Web Applications: Adding an Extra Layer of Trust

Multi-Factor Authentication (MFA) significantly enhances security by requiring users to provide more than one verification factor to access their account. Even if an attacker manages to steal a user's password, they will still need to bypass the additional factor. Common MFA methods include:

a) Something the user knows (Password): This is the traditional factor.

b) Something the user has (e.g., a one-time code sent to their phone via SMS or an authenticator app, a security key): This relies on the user possessing a physical device.

c) Something the user is (Biometrics, e.g., fingerprint or facial recognition): This relies on a unique biological characteristic.

Best Practices for Implementing MFA:

* Offer MFA as an Option (Ideally Enforce for Sensitive Accounts): Encourage all users to enable MFA, and consider enforcing it for accounts with elevated privileges or access to sensitive data.

* Support Multiple MFA Methods: Providing users with a choice of MFA methods (e.g., authenticator app, SMS, security key) can improve adoption and accessibility.

* Secure Enrollment Process: The process of setting up MFA should be secure and protect against attackers trying to enroll their own devices.

* Resilient Recovery Mechanisms: Provide secure ways for users to recover their accounts if they lose access to their MFA devices (e.g., backup codes).

* Clear User Guidance: Provide clear instructions and support to help users understand and set up MFA.

* Consider Step-Up Authentication: For particularly sensitive actions within the application, require users to re-authenticate with a second factor, even if they are already logged in.

Best Practices for "Remember Me" Functionality and Account Recovery: Convenience with Caution

"Remember Me" features and account recovery mechanisms offer convenience but need careful implementation to avoid introducing security vulnerabilities:

* Secure "Remember Me" Tokens: Instead of simply storing a username in a cookie, use secure, randomly generated, long-lived tokens. These tokens should be stored securely in the database and associated with the user. When a user returns, verify the token against the database. Consider using a two-token approach (a persistent token and a rotating secret) for

added security. Invalidate tokens on logout or after a certain period of inactivity.

* Secure Account Recovery (Password Reset):

    * Unique and Time-Limited Reset Tokens: When a user requests a password reset, generate a unique, cryptographically secure token with a limited lifespan.

    * Secure Token Delivery: Send the reset link containing the token to the user's verified email address.

    * Verify Token Validity: When the user clicks the link, verify the token against the database, ensuring it hasn't expired and hasn't already been used.

    * Prevent Token Reuse: Once a password has been successfully reset, invalidate the reset token.

    * Avoid Predictable Security Questions: If using security questions for account recovery, choose questions with non-obvious answers and provide guidance to users on selecting strong answers. Consider alternative methods like backup email addresses or phone numbers.

* Rate Limiting: Implement rate limiting on password reset requests to prevent brute-force attacks on the reset mechanism.

The Importance of a Holistic Approach to Authentication

Secure user management isn't just about one or two of these measures; it's about implementing a comprehensive and layered approach. Strong password policies, secure storage, robust session management, and the option (or enforcement) of MFA all work together to create a much more resilient authentication system.

As developers, we have a responsibility to our users to protect their accounts and the data associated with them. By understanding the common vulnerabilities and implementing these best practices, we can build authentication systems that are far more resistant to attack and provide a safer experience for everyone. In the next chapter, we'll shift our focus to another critical area: protecting sensitive data.

Chapter 6:

Sensitive Data Exposure: Protecting Your Users' Precious Information.

In today's digital world, our applications often handle a vast amount of sensitive data, from personal details and financial information to API keys and confidential business logic. If this data falls into the wrong hands, the consequences can be severe – for our users, our businesses, and our reputations.

This chapter is all about understanding what constitutes sensitive data, the various ways it can be exposed, and the crucial steps we, as developers, must take to protect it at every stage – from when it's collected to when it's stored and transmitted. Think of ourselves as guardians of this valuable information, and this chapter will equip us with the knowledge and tools to be effective protectors.

Identifying Sensitive Data in Web Applications: Knowing What to Guard

The first step in protecting sensitive data is to accurately identify what it is within our applications. This might seem obvious, but sometimes data that appears innocuous can become sensitive in the wrong context or when combined with other information. Here are some common categories of sensitive data we need to be mindful of:

Personally Identifiable Information (PII): This includes any information that can be used to identify an individual, such as names, addresses, email addresses, phone numbers, social security numbers (or equivalent national identification numbers), driver's license numbers, passport numbers, date of birth, and biometric data. Regulations like GDPR, CCPA, and others place strict requirements on how PII is handled.

Financial Information: This encompasses credit card numbers, bank account details, transaction history, and other financial records. Protecting this data is crucial to prevent fraud and financial loss.

Authentication Credentials: Usernames, passwords (especially the hashed versions), API keys, access tokens, and other secrets used for authentication and authorization must be rigorously protected.

Health Information: Medical records, diagnoses, treatment information, and any data related to an individual's health are highly sensitive and often subject to specific regulations like HIPAA.

Location Data: Precise location information can reveal a lot about an individual's habits and movements and is often considered sensitive.

Business Secrets and Intellectual Property: Confidential algorithms, trade secrets, internal business strategies, and other proprietary information are critical assets that need to be protected from unauthorized access.

Session Identifiers: While technically used for authentication, session IDs can be considered sensitive as their compromise can lead to account takeover.

It's important to conduct a thorough data mapping exercise for our applications to identify all types of sensitive data we collect, process, and store. Once we know what we need to protect, we can implement appropriate security measures.

Encryption Techniques for Data at Rest and in Transit: Locking Down Your Data

Encryption is a fundamental technique for protecting sensitive data. It involves converting data into an unreadable format (ciphertext) using an algorithm and a secret key. Only those with the correct key can decrypt the data back into its original form (plaintext). We need to apply encryption both when data is being transmitted (in transit) and when it's being stored (at rest).

Encryption in Transit (Using HTTPS/TLS): When data travels between a user's browser and our servers (or between different servers), it's vulnerable to interception. HTTPS (HTTP over TLS/SSL) is the standard protocol for securing web communication. It encrypts the data being transmitted, preventing eavesdropping and Man-in-the-Middle (MITM) attacks.

Key Practices for HTTPS:

Obtain a Valid SSL/TLS Certificate: Ensure you have a certificate from a trusted Certificate Authority (CA).

Enforce HTTPS: Configure your server to redirect all HTTP traffic to HTTPS.

Use Strong TLS Versions and Cipher Suites: Avoid outdated and insecure TLS versions (like SSLv3 or TLS 1.0/1.1) and choose strong, modern cipher suites.

Implement HSTS (HTTP Strict Transport Security): This HTTP security header instructs browsers to always communicate with your site over HTTPS, even if the user types http:// or clicks an old link.

Encryption at Rest: Data stored in our databases, file systems, or other storage mechanisms also needs protection. Even if our servers are physically secure, a data breach could still occur through compromised accounts or vulnerabilities. Encryption at rest helps to protect data even if the storage is accessed without authorization.

Key Considerations for Encryption at Rest:

Choose Appropriate Encryption Algorithms: Select strong, industry-standard encryption algorithms like AES (Advanced Encryption Standard).

Secure Key Management: The security of your encrypted data heavily relies on the security of your encryption keys. Store keys separately from the encrypted data and implement strict access controls. Consider using Hardware Security Modules (HSMs) or key management services for enhanced security.

Encrypt Only What's Necessary: While encrypting all sensitive data is generally recommended, consider the performance implications and legal requirements.

Database Encryption: Many modern database systems offer built-in encryption features for data at rest. Explore and utilize these capabilities.

Filesystem Encryption: For sensitive files, consider using filesystem-level encryption.

Secure Handling of API Keys, Secrets, and Credentials: Don't Let Your Keys Fall into the Wrong Hands

API keys, secret keys, and other credentials are like digital keys that grant access to various services and resources. If these are exposed, attackers can impersonate our applications or gain unauthorized access to sensitive functionalities. Here's how to handle them securely:

1) Never Hardcode Secrets Directly in Code: This is a major security no-no. Secrets embedded in code are easily discoverable if the code is compromised or even just viewed in a repository.

2) Use Environment Variables: Store sensitive configuration like API keys and database passwords as environment variables. This keeps them separate from your codebase.

3) Dedicated Secret Management Tools: For more complex applications, consider

using dedicated secret management tools like HashiCorp Vault, AWS Secrets Manager, Azure Key Vault, or Google Cloud Secret Manager. These tools provide secure storage, access control, rotation, and auditing of secrets.

4) Restrict Access: Apply the principle of least privilege to secrets. Only the components or services that absolutely need a particular secret should have access to it.

5) Regularly Rotate Secrets: Periodically change your API keys and other secrets to limit the impact if one is compromised. Many secret management tools offer automated rotation capabilities.

6) Avoid Storing Secrets in Version Control: Make sure to add secret files or configuration files containing secrets to your .gitignore (or equivalent) to prevent them from being committed to your version control system.

7) Secure Transmission of Secrets: When passing secrets between services, ensure

they are transmitted over secure channels (like HTTPS).

Data Masking and Tokenization Strategies: Protecting Sensitive Data in Non-Production Environments

Sometimes, we need to work with data that resembles production data in non-production environments (like development, testing, or staging). However, exposing real sensitive data in these environments increases the risk of accidental leaks or breaches. Data masking and tokenization are techniques to address this:

Data Masking: This involves obscuring or replacing sensitive data with realistic but non-sensitive substitutes. Techniques include:

Substitution: Replacing real values with fictional ones (e.g., replacing real names with fake names).

Shuffling: Randomly reordering values within a column.

Redaction: Removing or obscuring parts of the data (e.g., masking all but the last four digits of a credit card number).

Generalization: Replacing specific values with broader categories (e.g., replacing specific ages with age ranges).

Tokenization: This involves replacing sensitive data with non-sensitive placeholders called tokens. The actual sensitive data is stored securely in a separate vault, and the tokens can be used in non-production environments. If access to the real data is needed, the token can be de-tokenized under strict access control.

Compliance Considerations (e.g., GDPR, HIPAA) for Developers: Understanding Your Legal Obligations

Depending on the type of data our applications handle and the geographical location of our users, we may be subject to various data privacy regulations like GDPR (General Data Protection Regulation), CCPA (California Consumer Privacy Act), HIPAA (Health Insurance Portability and Accountability Act), and others. As developers, we need to be aware of the requirements imposed by these regulations and build our applications in a way that helps our organizations comply.

Key Areas of Compliance for Developers:

Data Minimization: Only collect and retain the data that is strictly necessary for the specified purpose.

Purpose Limitation: Only process data for the specific purposes for which it was collected.

Data Security: Implement appropriate technical and organizational measures to ensure the security of personal data, including encryption, access controls, and regular security assessments.

Data Integrity and Confidentiality: Ensure that personal data is accurate, complete, and protected against unauthorized access and disclosure.

Data Subject Rights: Understand and implement mechanisms to support data subject rights, such as the right to access, rectification, erasure, and data portability.

Privacy by Design and by Default: Integrate privacy considerations into the design of our applications from the outset and ensure that default settings are the most privacy-protective.

Logging and Auditing: Implement comprehensive logging and auditing mechanisms to track data access and processing activities.

It's crucial to work closely with legal and compliance teams within your organization to understand the specific regulations that apply to your applications and to ensure that your development practices align with these requirements.

The Importance of a Layered Approach to Data Protection

Protecting sensitive data is not a single step but a combination of multiple security controls implemented in layers. Encryption in transit and at rest, secure handling of secrets, data masking in non-production environments, and adherence to compliance regulations all contribute to a more robust security posture. If one layer fails, others are in place to provide continued protection.

As developers, we are on the front lines of protecting our users' sensitive information. By understanding the risks and implementing these best practices, we can build applications that are not only functional but also trustworthy and secure. In the next chapter, we'll delve into a more specific vulnerability: XML External Entities (XXE) attacks.

Chapter 7:

XML External Entities (XXE): Understanding and Preventing Attacks.

You might be thinking, "XML? Is that still a thing?" And while JSON has become incredibly popular, XML is still used in various systems, especially in older applications, data exchange formats, and some enterprise solutions. Ignoring the risks associated with XML processing can leave our applications wide open to attack.

In this chapter, we're going to dissect what XML External Entities are, how attackers can exploit them to gain unauthorized access to our systems, and the concrete steps we, as developers, need to take to parse XML securely and prevent these attacks. Think of this as learning about a hidden backdoor that might still exist in some of the systems we work with.

What are XML External Entities and How Can They Be Exploited? The Hidden Dangers Within XML

XML (Extensible Markup Language) is a markup language designed to be both human-readable and machine-readable. It allows for the definition of custom tags to structure and transport data. One of the features of XML is the ability to define entities, which are essentially placeholders for other content.

An XML External Entity (XXE) vulnerability arises when an XML parser is configured to process external entities, and an attacker can control the definition of these entities in the XML document being processed. These external entities can then be used to:

Access Local Files: An attacker can define an external entity that points to a file on the server's filesystem (using the file:// URI scheme). When the XML parser processes this entity, it will read the contents of the local file and potentially include it in the application's response or error messages, allowing the attacker to read sensitive information like configuration files, source code, or even password hashes.

Access Internal Network Resources: Similar to accessing local files, an attacker might be able to define an external entity that points to internal network resources (using HTTP or other URI schemes). This could allow them to probe the internal network, potentially discovering sensitive services or data.

Cause Denial of Service (DoS): An attacker could define an external entity that references a very large file or an infinitely recursive structure. When the XML parser tries to process this entity, it could consume excessive system resources (CPU, memory), leading to a denial of service.

Potentially Achieve Remote Code Execution (in some advanced scenarios): In certain, more complex configurations involving specific XML processors and libraries, XXE vulnerabilities could potentially be chained with other vulnerabilities to achieve remote code execution on the server.

Common XXE Attack Scenarios in Web Applications: Where the Backdoor Might Be Found

XXE vulnerabilities can lurk in various parts of a web application that process XML data. Here are some common scenarios to be aware of:

SOAP APIs: Many older web services still use SOAP (Simple Object Access Protocol), which relies on XML for message formatting. If the SOAP implementation on the server-side processes XML without proper XXE prevention, it can be vulnerable.

File Uploads: Applications that allow users to upload XML files (e.g., for configuration, data import, or document processing) are potential targets if they parse these files without disabling external entity processing.

XML Data Exchange: Applications that receive XML data from other systems or partners (e.g., through APIs or data feeds) need to ensure they are parsing this data securely.

Server-Side XML Processing for Templating or Configuration: Some applications might use XML for server-side templating or configuration files. If these files are processed dynamically based on user input or external data, they could be vulnerable to XXE.

Best Practices for Parsing XML Securely in Different Programming Languages: Closing the Backdoor

The key to preventing XXE attacks is to disable the processing of external entities in your XML parsers. Most XML parsing libraries in various programming languages provide settings or options to control this behavior. We need to ensure that these settings are configured securely.

Here are some best practices for common programming languages:

Java:

When using javax.xml.parsers.DocumentBuilderFactory or javax.xml.parsers.SAXParserFactory, explicitly set the following features to false before creating a parser:

```
factory.setFeature("http://apache.org/xml/feature
s/disallow-doctype-decl", true); // Disallow
DOCTYPE declarations
factory.setFeature("http://xml.org/sax/features/ex
ternal-general-entities", false); // Disable
external general entities
factory.setFeature("http://xml.org/sax/features/ex
ternal-parameter-entities", false); // Disable
external parameter entities
factory.setFeature("http://apache.org/xml/feature
s/nonvalidating/load-external-dtd", false); //
Disable external DTD loading
factory.setXIncludeAware(false); // Disable
XInclude processing
```

Python:
When using libraries like xml.etree.ElementTree, lxml, or xml.dom.minidom, avoid using functions or configurations that automatically resolve external entities. For example, with lxml, you

can use the no_network=True option in the XMLParser:

```
from lxml import etree

xml_content                                    =
"<root><data>&evil;</data></root>"
evil_entity = "<!DOCTYPE root [ <!ENTITY
evil SYSTEM 'file:///etc/passwd'> ]>"
parsed_xml    =    etree.fromstring(evil_entity    +
xml_content,
etree.XMLParser(no_network=True))
data = parsed_xml.findtext('data')
print(data) # This should not print the content of
/etc/passwd
```

Be cautious with default settings, as some older versions or configurations might have external entity processing enabled by default.

PHP:
When using functions like simplexml_load_string() or DOMDocument::loadXML(), you can disable external entity loading:

```
libxml_disable_entity_loader(true);
```

```php
$xml_content                    =                  '<?xml
version="1.0"?><!DOCTYPE foo [ <!ENTITY
xxe       SYSTEM        "file:///etc/passwd">
]><foo>&xxe;</foo>';
$xml = simplexml_load_string($xml_content);
echo $xml; // This should not output the content
of /etc/passwd

$dom = new DOMDocument();
$dom->loadXML($xml_content,
LIBXML_NOENT | LIBXML_DTDLOAD); //
Avoid these flags
echo $dom->textContent;
```

Ensure libxml_disable_entity_loader(true) is called before parsing any XML from untrusted sources.

.NET (C#):

When using XmlReaderSettings, XmlDocument, or XmlTextReader, configure them to disable external entity resolution:

```csharp
XmlReaderSettings settings = new
XmlReaderSettings();
```

```
settings.DtdProcessing                          =
DtdProcessing.Prohibit;    //   Disallow   DTD
processing
settings.XmlResolver = null; // Prevent resolving
external entities

using          (XmlReader       reader       =
XmlReader.Create(xmlFile, settings))
{
  // Process XML
}

XmlDocument doc = new XmlDocument();
doc.XmlResolver  =  null;  //  Prevent  resolving
external entities
doc.Load(xmlFile);
```

JavaScript (Server-Side with libraries like xml2js):
- Review the documentation of your chosen XML parsing library for options to disable external entity processing or secure parsing modes. Be particularly cautious

with older or less maintained libraries that might have insecure defaults.

Disabling External Entity Resolution: The Primary Defense

As highlighted in the language-specific best practices, the most crucial step in preventing XXE attacks is to disable the XML parser's ability to resolve external entities altogether. This effectively removes the attack vector by preventing the parser from accessing external files or network resources.

Input Validation for XML Data: Another Layer of Protection

While disabling external entity resolution is the primary defense, it's still a good practice to validate the structure and content of the XML data you are processing. This can help to detect and reject potentially malicious XML documents even before they are fully parsed.

- Schema Validation: If you expect XML documents to conform to a specific schema (e.g., using XSD), validate the incoming XML against that schema. This can help to identify unexpected elements or attributes that might be part of an attack.

- Content Validation: Validate the values within the XML elements and attributes to ensure they meet your application's requirements.

However, remember that input validation alone is not sufficient to prevent XXE. An attacker might be able to craft a valid XML document that still exploits external entities if the parser is configured to process them. Disabling external entity resolution is the essential first step.

The Importance of Staying Updated and Reviewing Configurations

XML parsing libraries and their default configurations can change over time. It's important to stay updated with the latest security recommendations for the libraries you are using and to regularly review your XML parsing code and configurations to ensure that external entity processing remains disabled.

In Conclusion:

XXE vulnerabilities might seem like a niche issue, but they can provide attackers with a significant foothold into our systems, allowing them to access sensitive local files, probe internal networks, cause denial of service, and in some cases, even achieve remote code execution.

As developers, we need to be aware of this potential vulnerability, especially when dealing with applications that process XML data, even if it's not the primary data format. By understanding what XML External Entities are and, more importantly, by implementing the best practice of disabling external entity resolution in our XML parsers, we can effectively close this often-overlooked backdoor.

Always remember to consult the security documentation for the specific XML parsing libraries you are using in your chosen programming languages. Ensure that you are using the recommended secure configurations and staying updated with the latest security advice. While input validation of XML data can provide an additional layer of defense, it should not be relied upon as the primary protection against XXE attacks. Disabling external entities is the key to secure XML processing.

By taking these precautions, we can ensure that our applications are not vulnerable to this potentially severe class of attacks and that we are handling XML data in a secure and responsible manner. In the next chapter, we'll shift gears and discuss another critical aspect of web application security: Broken Access Control.

Chapter 8:

Broken Access Control: Ensuring Proper Authorization.

We've talked about authentication (verifying who a user is), but access control, or authorization, is about determining what a user is allowed to do once they're authenticated. It's the gatekeeper that decides who gets to see what data and perform which actions.

Think of it like this: getting a key to a building (authentication) doesn't mean you have access to every room inside (authorization). Broken access control occurs when these permissions aren't properly enforced, allowing users to access resources or perform actions they shouldn't be able to. This can lead to everything from viewing other users' private data to performing administrative functions without proper authorization.

In this chapter, we're going to explore the different types of access control vulnerabilities, the common mistakes developers make that lead to them, and the robust strategies we can implement to ensure proper authorization in our web applications.

Understanding Different Types of Access Control Vulnerabilities: When the Gates Aren't Locked

Broken access control can manifest in various ways, often stemming from flawed design or implementation of authorization mechanisms. Here are some common types of vulnerabilities we need to be aware of:

- Insecure Direct Object References (IDOR): This occurs when an application exposes a direct reference to an internal implementation object, such as a file, database record, or API endpoint, in a way that allows an attacker to bypass authorization checks and access other users' objects by simply modifying the reference. For example, accessing example.com/user/123 to view user ID 123's profile, and then simply changing 123 to 456 to view another user's profile without proper authorization.

- Missing Function Level Access Control: This happens when the application doesn't properly enforce authorization at the function level. For example, administrative functions might be accessible simply by guessing the URL or by manipulating parameters, without the application verifying if the user has the necessary administrative privileges.

- Horizontal Privilege Escalation: This occurs when a user is able to gain access to resources or perform actions that belong to another user with the same level of privileges. In our earlier example, viewing another user's profile via IDOR is a form of horizontal privilege escalation.

- Vertical Privilege Escalation: This is more severe and happens when a lower-privileged user is able to gain access to resources or perform actions that are reserved for higher-privileged users (e.g., a regular user gaining administrative access).

- Metadata Manipulation: Attackers might try to manipulate metadata, such as user roles or permissions stored in cookies or hidden fields, to gain unauthorized access. If the application trusts this manipulated metadata without server-side verification, it can lead to broken access control.

- CORS Misconfiguration: Cross-Origin Resource Sharing (CORS) is a mechanism that allows web pages from one domain to request resources from another domain. If CORS is misconfigured, it can allow unauthorized origins to access sensitive resources. While not strictly an access control vulnerability within the application itself, it's a related issue that can lead to data exposure.

- Path Traversal (Covered in XXE but related to file access): While we discussed path traversal in the context of XXE, it's also a form of broken access control where an attacker can manipulate file paths to access files outside of their intended scope.

Implementing Role-Based Access Control (RBAC) and Attribute-Based Access Control (ABAC): Structuring Permissions

To effectively manage access control, we often rely on structured models like Role-Based

Access Control (RBAC) and Attribute-Based Access Control (ABAC):

Role-Based Access Control (RBAC): This is a common and effective model where permissions are associated with roles, and users are assigned to one or more roles. When a user tries to access a resource or perform an action, the application checks if their assigned role(s) have the necessary permissions.

Key Concepts in RBAC:

Roles: Collections of permissions (e.g., "administrator," "editor," "viewer").

Permissions: Rights to perform specific actions on specific resources (e.g., "read user profile," "edit article," "delete user").

Users: Individuals who interact with the application.

Role Assignment: The process of assigning roles to users.

Permission Assignment: The process of assigning permissions to roles.

Benefits of RBAC: Simplifies access management, provides a clear and auditable structure, and makes it easier to manage permissions for groups of users.

Attribute-Based Access Control (ABAC): This is a more flexible and granular model where access decisions are based on a set of attributes associated with the user, the resource being accessed, and the environment.

Key Concepts in ABAC:

User Attributes: Characteristics of the user (e.g., role, group membership, security clearance).

Resource Attributes: Properties of the resource being accessed (e.g., file type, creation date, sensitivity level).

Environment Attributes: Contextual factors (e.g., time of day, location, access method).

Policies: Rules that define whether access is allowed based on the evaluation of these attributes.

Benefits of ABAC: Offers fine-grained control over access, can handle complex authorization scenarios, and is more dynamic and adaptable to changing requirements.

Preventing Insecure Direct Object References (IDOR): Don't Expose Internal IDs

IDOR vulnerabilities are prevalent and can be easily exploited. Here's how to prevent them:

- Use Indirect References: Instead of exposing internal IDs (like database primary keys) directly in URLs or API parameters, use indirect, opaque references that are not easily guessable or predictable. These references should be mapped to the actual internal IDs on the server-side.

- Implement Proper Authorization Checks: Before allowing a user to access an object based on a reference (direct or indirect), always verify that the user has the necessary permissions to access that specific object. Don't assume that because they are authenticated, they can access anything.

- Avoid Predictable Identifiers: If you must use some form of identifier in the client-side, make sure it's not easily predictable or sequential. Use UUIDs (Universally Unique Identifiers) or other random, non-guessable strings.
- Consider Scope: When checking access, consider the scope of the resource. For example, a user might be allowed to view their own profile but not the profiles of others.

Secure API Design for Authorization: Protecting Your Endpoints

APIs are often a prime target for broken access control vulnerabilities. Here's how to design them with security in mind:

Implement Authorization at the API Endpoint Level: Every API endpoint should enforce proper authorization checks to ensure that only authorized users or applications can access it.

Use Authorization Headers/Tokens: For APIs, authentication and authorization information is often passed in headers (e.g., using Bearer tokens). Ensure these tokens are validated on the server for every request.

Follow the Principle of Least Privilege: Grant API clients only the necessary permissions they need to perform their intended tasks. Avoid giving broad or unnecessary access.

Be Careful with Path Parameters: Just like with IDOR in web pages, be cautious about relying on path parameters to identify resources without proper authorization checks.

Consider Using Framework-Level Authorization Mechanisms: Many web frameworks provide built-in features or libraries for handling API authentication and authorization (e.g., JWT-based authentication and role-based access control). Leverage these tools.

Testing and Auditing Access Control Mechanisms: Verify Your Gates Are Locked

It's not enough to implement access control mechanisms; we also need to thoroughly test and audit them to ensure they are working correctly and haven't introduced any vulnerabilities.

Manual Testing: Perform manual testing with different user roles and privileges to try and access resources or perform actions that should be restricted. Try manipulating IDs and parameters to see if you can bypass authorization checks.

Automated Testing: Incorporate automated tests into your CI/CD pipeline that specifically target access control vulnerabilities. These tests can verify that different roles can access the correct resources and that unauthorized access is denied.

Code Reviews: Have your code reviewed by other developers with a focus on identifying potential access control flaws.

Security Audits and Penetration Testing: Engage security professionals to conduct regular security audits and penetration testing of your application, specifically focusing on access control weaknesses.

Logging and Monitoring: Implement comprehensive logging of access attempts, especially failed ones and attempts to access restricted resources. Monitor these logs for suspicious activity.

The Importance of Server-Side Enforcement: Never Trust the Client

A fundamental principle of secure access control is to always enforce authorization on the server-side. Never rely solely on client-side checks (e.g., hiding UI elements or disabling buttons) to restrict access. Attackers can easily bypass these client-side controls by manipulating requests directly. The server must always verify that the authenticated user has the necessary permissions to access the requested resource or perform the requested action.

In Conclusion:

Broken access control is a critical vulnerability that can lead to severe security breaches. By understanding the different ways it can manifest and implementing robust authorization mechanisms like RBAC and ABAC, using indirect references to prevent IDOR, designing secure APIs, and thoroughly testing our access controls, we can build web applications where the gates are truly locked. Remember the cardinal rule: always enforce access control on the server-side and never trust the client. By adopting a security-first mindset in our design and implementation of authorization, we can ensure that our users can only access the data and functionality they are explicitly permitted to, protecting sensitive information and preventing unauthorized actions. In the next chapter, we'll turn our attention to another common source of vulnerabilities: Security Misconfiguration.

Chapter 9:

Security Misconfiguration: Hardening Your Web Application Environment.

You might have the most securely coded application in the world, with robust authentication and authorization, and all the injection vulnerabilities patched up. But if your underlying environment – your servers, your frameworks, your configurations – isn't properly secured, you're still leaving the door wide open for attackers.

Security misconfiguration is a broad category that encompasses a wide range of common mistakes in setting up and maintaining our web application infrastructure. These misconfigurations can expose sensitive information, grant unintended access, and create pathways for various attacks. Think of it like building that secure house we talked about, but leaving the windows unlocked or using easily picked locks on the doors.

In this chapter, we're going to explore the common configuration errors that can lead to security vulnerabilities, discuss secure deployment practices, the importance of proper error handling and logging, the critical need for keeping our software up-to-date, and how to securely configure our web servers and application frameworks.

Common Configuration Errors That Lead to Security Vulnerabilities: The Low-Hanging Fruit for Attackers

Attackers often look for the easiest way in, and misconfigurations provide just that – low-hanging fruit that requires minimal effort to exploit. Here are some common configuration errors we need to avoid:

- Default Passwords: Leaving default usernames and passwords on administrative interfaces, databases, or other components is a critical mistake. Attackers often have lists of default credentials and will try them first.

- Unnecessary Features Enabled: Enabling features, services, or HTTP methods that aren't required by your application increases the attack surface. Each enabled feature is a potential entry point for vulnerabilities. For example, leaving unnecessary administrative interfaces accessible or enabling dangerous HTTP methods like TRACE or PUT on public-facing servers.

- Verbose Error Messages: Displaying detailed error messages to users in production environments can reveal sensitive information about your application's internal workings, file paths, database structure, or the versions of software you're using. This information can be invaluable to attackers.

- Unpatched Software: Using outdated versions of operating systems, web servers, application frameworks, libraries, and plugins that contain known security vulnerabilities is a significant risk. Attackers actively scan for and exploit these known weaknesses.

- Insecure Default Configurations: Many software packages come with default configurations that prioritize ease of use over security. These defaults often need to be reviewed and hardened for a production environment. For example, default file permissions that are too permissive.

- Exposed Sensitive Directories: Leaving administrative or backup directories publicly accessible can allow attackers to find sensitive information or even gain control over parts of your application.

- Missing Security Headers: As we'll discuss in detail later, not implementing crucial HTTP security headers leaves your application vulnerable to various client-side attacks like XSS and clickjacking.

- Cloud Storage Misconfigurations: Incorrectly configured permissions on cloud storage buckets (like AWS S3, Azure Blob Storage, Google Cloud Storage) can lead to the public exposure of sensitive data.

Secure Deployment Practices: Minimizing Your Attack Surface

How we deploy our applications has a significant impact on their security. Secure deployment practices aim to minimize the attack surface and ensure a hardened environment:

Principle of Least Privilege: Run your application processes with the minimum necessary user and group privileges. If a process is compromised, the attacker's ability to cause damage will be limited by these reduced privileges.

Secure Server Hardening: Harden your operating systems by disabling unnecessary services, closing unused ports, and applying security patches promptly.

Network Segmentation: Isolate your web servers, application servers, and database servers into separate network segments with strict firewall rules controlling traffic between them. This limits the impact if one segment is compromised.

Immutable Infrastructure: Consider using immutable infrastructure where servers are replaced rather than updated. This reduces configuration drift and makes it easier to ensure a consistent and secure environment.

Infrastructure as Code (IaC): Use IaC tools (like Terraform, CloudFormation, Ansible) to define and manage your infrastructure. This allows for version control, repeatability, and easier auditing of your configurations.

Regular Security Audits of Infrastructure: Just like your application code, your infrastructure configurations should be regularly audited for security weaknesses.

Proper Error Handling and Logging for Security: Balancing User Experience and Security

How we handle errors and log events is crucial for both user experience and security. We need to strike a balance between providing helpful information to users and not revealing too much to potential attackers:

- Generic Error Messages in Production: In production environments, display generic error messages to users (e.g., "An unexpected error occurred"). Avoid showing detailed stack traces or internal error information that could expose sensitive details.

- Detailed Logging on the Server: Implement comprehensive logging on the server-side, recording important events such as authentication attempts, access to sensitive resources, errors, and security-related events.
- Secure Log Storage and Access: Store logs securely and restrict access to them to authorized personnel only. Logs can contain sensitive information and can be invaluable for incident response and forensic analysis.
- Log Monitoring and Alerting: Implement systems to monitor logs for suspicious activity, unusual patterns, or security incidents, and set up alerts to notify security teams of potential threats.

Keeping Software and Dependencies Up-to-Date: Patch Management for Developers

Using outdated software is like leaving known vulnerabilities unpatched. Attackers actively look for systems running vulnerable versions of operating systems, web servers, frameworks, libraries, and plugins.

- Maintain an Inventory: Keep a detailed inventory of all software and dependencies used in your application.
- Regular Vulnerability Scanning: Use tools to regularly scan your infrastructure and dependencies for known security vulnerabilities.
- Prompt Patching: Have a process in place to promptly apply security patches and updates as soon as they are released. Prioritize patching critical vulnerabilities.
- Automated Updates (with Caution): Consider automating updates where appropriate, but ensure thorough testing in a staging environment before deploying to production.
- Dependency Management Tools: Use dependency management tools (like npm, Maven, pip) that can help identify and update vulnerable dependencies.

- Stay Informed: Subscribe to security mailing lists and monitor security advisories for the software you use.

Secure Configuration of Web Servers and Application Frameworks: Hardening Your Foundation

Your web server (like Apache or Nginx) and your application framework (like Spring, Django, Express.js) have numerous configuration options that can impact security. It's crucial to review and harden these configurations:

Web Server Hardening:

- Disable Unnecessary Modules: Disable any server modules that are not required by your application.
- Restrict HTTP Methods: Only enable the necessary HTTP methods (e.g., GET, POST) and disable others like PUT, DELETE, and TRACE on public-facing servers.
- Configure Directory Listing: Disable directory listing to prevent attackers from

browsing the contents of your server directories.

- Set Appropriate Timeouts: Configure appropriate timeouts for connections to prevent denial-of-service attacks.
- Limit Request Size: Set limits on the size of incoming requests to prevent large uploads that could exhaust server resources.
- Control Access with Virtual Hosts and Configuration Directives: Use virtual hosts and access control directives (like .htaccess for Apache or location blocks for Nginx) to restrict access to sensitive areas of your application.
- Application Framework Security Configuration:
- Session Management: Configure secure session management as discussed in Chapter 5.
- CSRF Protection: Enable built-in Cross-Site Request Forgery (CSRF) protection mechanisms provided by your framework.

- XSS Protection: Utilize framework features to prevent Cross-Site Scripting (XSS) vulnerabilities, such as template engines with automatic output escaping.
- Security Headers: Configure your framework to send appropriate HTTP security headers.
- Database Security: Configure secure database connections and follow the principle of least privilege for database user accounts.

Framework-Specific Security Best Practices: Familiarize yourself with the security best practices and configuration guidelines specific to the framework you are using.

The Ongoing Nature of Secure Configuration

Security misconfiguration isn't a one-time fix; it's an ongoing process. As our applications and infrastructure evolve, we need to continuously review and adjust our configurations to maintain a secure environment. Regular security assessments and adherence to best practices are essential to prevent these often-overlooked vulnerabilities from becoming our weakest link.

In the next chapter, we'll delve into the world of Cross-Site Scripting (XSS) attacks and how to protect our users from client-side threats.

Chapter 10:

Cross-Site Scripting (XSS): Protecting Against Client-Side Attacks.

Up until now, we've focused a lot on server-side vulnerabilities. But XSS is a different beast – it's a client-side attack that targets the users of our web applications. And while it might not directly compromise our servers in the same way as injection flaws, it can have serious consequences for our users and our application's reputation.

Think of XSS as an attacker injecting malicious code – usually in the form of JavaScript – into web pages that other users view. When the victim's browser executes this malicious script, it can lead to a variety of nasty outcomes, from stealing their session cookies and hijacking their accounts to defacing websites or redirecting them to malicious sites.

In this chapter, we're going to understand the different types of XSS attacks, how these vulnerabilities arise in our frontend and backend code, the crucial techniques for preventing them (like input sanitization and output encoding), and the powerful role that Content Security Policy (CSP) plays in mitigating XSS risks.

Understanding Different Types of XSS Attacks (Reflected, Stored, DOM-based): The Many Faces of Client-Side Injection

XSS attacks can be broadly categorized into three main types, depending on how the malicious script gets into the web page and where it originates:

- Reflected XSS (Non-Persistent): This is the most common type. In a reflected XSS attack, the malicious script is embedded in a URL or submitted through a form. The server then includes this unsanitized input in its response, and the victim's browser executes the script. The script is not stored on the server; it's "reflected" back to the user. Common scenarios include malicious links sent via email or social media.

Example: A search functionality where the search term is displayed on the results page without proper encoding. An attacker could craft a URL like example.com/search?query=<script>alert('Hacked!')</script>. If a user clicks this link, the alert will be executed in their browser.

- Stored XSS (Persistent): In this more dangerous type, the malicious script is stored on the server (e.g., in a database, comment section, forum post, or user profile). When other users view the page containing this stored script, their browsers execute it. Because the payload is persistent, it can affect multiple users over time.

Example: A comment section on a blog where users can enter HTML. If the application doesn't sanitize the input, an attacker can post a comment containing a <script> tag. Every user who views that comment will have the script executed in their browser.

- DOM-based XSS: This type of XSS occurs entirely in the client-side code (JavaScript) and doesn't necessarily involve the server sending malicious data in the initial response. The vulnerability arises when the client-side script takes data from a controllable source (like the URL fragment #, or other parts of the

DOM) and passes it to a sink (a function that can execute JavaScript, like eval() or setting innerHTML) without proper sanitization.

Example: A website with JavaScript that reads a parameter from the URL fragment (window.location.hash) and uses it to update the page content using innerHTML. An attacker could craft a URL like example.com/#<img src=x onerror=alert('Hacked!')>. The browser doesn't send the fragment to the server, but the client-side script processes it, leading to the execution of the malicious script.

How XSS Vulnerabilities Arise in Frontend and Backend Code: The Pathways for Malicious Scripts

XSS vulnerabilities typically occur when we, as developers, fail to properly handle user-provided data. This can happen in both our frontend (client-side JavaScript) and backend code:

- Backend Code: The backend is often responsible for receiving user input and rendering web pages. If the backend doesn't sanitize user input before including it in the HTML response, it can create opportunities for reflected or stored XSS. This includes data from form submissions, URL parameters, database records, and any other source of user-controlled content.

- Frontend Code (JavaScript): Client-side JavaScript can also introduce XSS vulnerabilities, particularly with DOM-based XSS. If JavaScript code processes user-controlled data from the DOM (like the URL, cookies, or other parts of the HTML) and uses it in a way that can execute scripts without proper sanitization, it can lead to attacks.

Effective Input Sanitization and Output Encoding Techniques: Our Primary Weapons Against XSS

The core strategies for preventing XSS are input sanitization and output encoding. While they sound similar, they serve different purposes and are often used in conjunction:

- Input Sanitization: This involves cleaning user-provided data to remove or modify potentially malicious content before it's stored or processed. The goal is to make the input safe for our application's logic. However, aggressive sanitization can sometimes break legitimate user input, so it needs to be done carefully and contextually.

Example: Removing HTML tags from a comment field if only plain text is expected.

Output Encoding (or Escaping): This is the more crucial defense against XSS. It involves converting potentially dangerous characters in user-provided data into a safe format when it's being rendered in the HTML. This ensures that the browser interprets the data as text, not as executable code. The specific encoding needed depends on where the data is being inserted in the HTML context (e.g., HTML tags, attributes, JavaScript context, CSS context, URL context).

- HTML Entity Encoding: For inserting data within HTML tags, characters like <, >, &, ", and ' should be replaced with their corresponding HTML entities (<, >, &, ", ').

- JavaScript Encoding: When inserting data within <script> tags or JavaScript event handlers, different encoding rules apply. You might need to escape characters like backslashes, single quotes, double quotes, etc., to prevent them from breaking the JavaScript syntax.
- URL Encoding: When embedding user data in URLs, special characters need to be URL-encoded to prevent them from being misinterpreted.
- CSS Encoding: When inserting data into CSS styles, certain characters might need to be escaped to prevent malicious styles.

Key Principle: Always encode on output, in the specific context where the data is being rendered. Input sanitization can be a helpful supplementary measure, but it should not be relied upon as the primary defense against XSS. Using Content Security Policy (CSP) to Mitigate XSS: A Powerful Browser-Side Control

Content Security Policy (CSP) is an HTTP security header that provides an extra layer of defense against XSS attacks (and other client-side threats). CSP allows us to define a policy that tells the browser which sources of content (scripts, styles, images, fonts, etc.) are considered trusted for our web page. The browser will then block any content that violates this policy.

How CSP Works:

We send a Content-Security-Policy header (or a <meta> tag in the <head> section) in our server's response. This header contains directives that specify the allowed sources for different types of resources. For example:

default-src 'self': Allows loading resources only from the same origin as the document.

script-src 'self' https://trusted-cdn.com: Allows loading scripts only from the same origin and from https://trusted-cdn.com. Inline scripts (within <script> tags) are blocked by default with this directive.

style-src 'self': Allows loading stylesheets only from the same origin. Inline styles (within

<style> tags or style attributes) are blocked by default.

img-src *: Allows loading images from any source.

object-src 'none': Disallows loading plugins like Flash.

Benefits of CSP:

- Reduces the Impact of XSS: Even if an attacker manages to inject malicious script into the page, CSP can prevent the browser from executing it if the script's origin doesn't match the allowed sources.
- Defense in Depth: CSP acts as an additional security layer, even if we make mistakes in output encoding.
- Mitigates Other Attacks: CSP can also help prevent other types of attacks, such as clickjacking and data injection.

Implementing CSP:

Implementing CSP effectively requires careful planning and configuration. You'll need to identify all the legitimate sources of content for your website and create a policy that allows them while restricting everything else. It's often best to start with a restrictive policy and gradually loosen it as needed, monitoring for any violations reported by the browser. The Content-Security-Policy-Report-Only header can be used to test policies without blocking content initially.

Best Practices for Handling User-Generated Content: Extra Care Required

Applications that allow users to submit and display content (like comments, forum posts, profiles) require extra vigilance against stored XSS. Here are some best practices:

- Choose a Safe Markup Language (if needed): If you need to allow some formatting, consider using a safe markup language like Markdown and parsing it on the server-side to generate safe HTML.
- Strict Output Encoding: For any user-generated content that is displayed as HTML, apply rigorous output encoding appropriate for the HTML context.
- Consider Content Sanitization Libraries: Many programming languages have libraries specifically designed to sanitize

HTML, removing potentially malicious elements and attributes while preserving safe ones. Use these with caution and ensure they are up-to-date.

- Use CSP Effectively: Implement a strict CSP that limits the capabilities of any user-generated content, such as disallowing inline scripts and restricting script sources.
- Regularly Audit User-Generated Content: Implement mechanisms to monitor and audit user-generated content for suspicious activity or potential XSS payloads.

In Conclusion:

Cross-Site Scripting is a persistent and dangerous threat to web applications. By understanding the different types of XSS, how they arise, and implementing robust defenses like meticulous output encoding in the correct context and leveraging the power of Content Security Policy, we can significantly reduce the risk to our users. Remember that preventing XSS requires a defense-in-depth approach, combining secure coding practices with browser-level security controls. In the next chapter, we'll explore another often-overlooked vulnerability: Insecure Deserialization.

Chapter 11:

Insecure Deserialization: Exploiting Object Handling.

This might sound a bit technical, but bear with me. Serialization and deserialization are common processes in web applications, especially in distributed systems and when dealing with caching or session management. However, if not handled carefully, these processes can create openings for attackers to execute arbitrary code on our servers.

Think of serialization as the process of converting an object (a piece of data with associated methods and properties in our code) into a format that can be easily stored or transmitted (like a string of bytes). Deserialization is the reverse process – taking that stored or transmitted format and reconstructing the original object in memory. The danger arises when the data being deserialized is untrusted and can be manipulated by an attacker.

In this chapter, we're going to explore what object serialization and deserialization are, the common vulnerabilities associated with insecure deserialization, how attackers can exploit these flaws, and the crucial steps we need to take to prevent them in our code across different programming languages.

What is Object Serialization and Deserialization? The Conversion Process

In many programming languages, objects can be converted into a stream of bytes for various purposes:

- Storing in Databases or Caches: Objects can be serialized to be stored in databases or caching systems like Redis or Memcached.
- Transmitting Over Networks: In distributed systems or when making remote procedure calls (RPC), objects might be serialized to be sent across the network.
- Session Management: Some web frameworks serialize user session objects to store them in cookies or server-side session stores.

Deserialization is the process of taking this stream of bytes and reconstructing the original object in the application's memory. The key vulnerability occurs when the data being deserialized comes from an untrusted source (like user input, cookies, or external systems) and has been tampered with by an attacker.

Common Vulnerabilities Associated with Insecure Deserialization: The Hidden Dangers

The risks of insecure deserialization can be severe because the act of deserializing untrusted data can lead to unexpected and dangerous code execution. Here's why:

* Object State Manipulation: Attackers can manipulate the serialized data to alter the state of the deserialized object. This might allow them to bypass security checks, escalate privileges, or access sensitive data.

Gadget Chains and Arbitrary Code Execution: Many programming languages have libraries and classes (often called "gadgets") that, when their methods are invoked in a specific sequence during deserialization, can lead to arbitrary code execution on the server. Attackers can craft malicious serialized payloads that trigger these gadget chains, effectively allowing them to run any code they want on the server.

Denial of Service (DoS): Attackers can create malicious serialized payloads that consume excessive resources (CPU, memory) during deserialization, leading to a denial of service.

Preventing Insecure Deserialization in Different Programming Languages: Secure Handling Strategies

The best way to prevent insecure deserialization vulnerabilities is to avoid deserializing untrusted data whenever possible. If you must deserialize data from an external source, here are some crucial strategies to follow, keeping in mind that specific implementations will vary by language and framework:

- Avoid Native Serialization Formats with Untrusted Data: Many languages have built-in serialization formats (like Java's ObjectOutputStream, Python's pickle, PHP's unserialize). These formats often don't provide strong integrity checks and can be vulnerable to manipulation. Avoid using them to deserialize data from untrusted sources.

- Use Signed Serialization: If you must use a native serialization format, ensure that the serialized data is cryptographically signed. Before deserializing, verify the signature to ensure the data hasn't been tampered with. However, even with signing, vulnerabilities might still exist in the deserialization process itself.
- Use Safer Data Formats: Consider using safer data formats like JSON or Protocol Buffers for data exchange. These formats typically don't include the ability to arbitrarily instantiate objects and execute code during parsing. If you use them, ensure you are using secure parsing libraries that are regularly updated.
- Implement Strong Input Validation: Regardless of the serialization format, validate the structure and content of the data being deserialized to ensure it conforms to your expected schema. This

can help prevent the deserialization of unexpected or malicious payloads.

- Isolate Deserialization Environments: If you absolutely must deserialize untrusted data, consider doing it in a sandboxed or isolated environment with limited privileges to minimize the impact of any potential exploitation.
- Principle of Least Privilege: Run your application with the minimum necessary privileges to limit the damage an attacker can do if they manage to exploit a deserialization vulnerability.
- Keep Dependencies Up-to-Date: Ensure that your serialization and deserialization libraries, as well as your entire application stack, are up-to-date with the latest security patches.

Language-Specific Considerations:

Java: Insecure deserialization has been a significant source of vulnerabilities in Java applications. Avoid using ObjectInputStream.readObject() with untrusted data. If you must, implement robust input validation and consider using safer serialization libraries or signing mechanisms. Be aware of known "gadget chains" in popular Java libraries.

Python: The pickle module in Python is known to be insecure when used with untrusted data. Avoid using pickle.load() with data from external sources. Consider using json or marshal (though marshal is not intended for general-purpose serialization) with appropriate validation.

PHP: The unserialize() function in PHP has been the source of many security vulnerabilities. Avoid using it with untrusted data. If necessary, carefully validate the structure of the serialized data and consider using safer alternatives like JSON or signing mechanisms. Be aware of potential object injection vulnerabilities through unserialize().

.NET (C#): Be cautious when using BinaryFormatter or ObjectStateFormatter with untrusted data. Consider using DataContractSerializer or JsonSerializer with strict schema validation. Signing the serialized data can also add a layer of protection.

JavaScript (Node.js): While JavaScript itself doesn't have a built-in serialization format as dangerous as pickle or unserialize, be cautious when using libraries that serialize and deserialize objects, especially if the data originates from untrusted sources. Use JSON.stringify() and JSON.parse() with careful validation.

Secure Alternatives to Serialization: Choosing Safer Paths

Given the inherent risks associated with deserializing untrusted data, it's often better to explore safer alternatives for data exchange and storage:

JSON (JavaScript Object Notation): A lightweight and widely used data format that is generally safer than native serialization formats as it doesn't inherently include code execution capabilities during parsing. However, be sure to use secure JSON parsing libraries.

Protocol Buffers: A language-neutral, platform-neutral, extensible mechanism for serializing structured data. They are designed with efficiency and safety in mind.

Database Storage: For persistent data, storing objects in a structured format in a database and querying them as needed is often a safer approach than serializing and deserializing entire object graphs.

Auditing Code for Deserialization Vulnerabilities: Vigilance is Key

It's crucial to audit our codebases for any instances where untrusted data is being deserialized using potentially vulnerable methods. This includes reviewing how data is handled in:

API Endpoints: Pay close attention to data received from clients that is being deserialized.

Session Management: Check how session data is being serialized and deserialized.

Caching Mechanisms: Review how objects are stored in and retrieved from caches.

Inter-Service Communication: Examine how data is exchanged between different parts of your application or with external services.

In Conclusion:

Insecure deserialization is a subtle but highly dangerous vulnerability that can lead to arbitrary code execution and complete server compromise. The best defense is to avoid deserializing untrusted data using native serialization formats whenever possible. If you must, employ strong preventative measures like using safer data formats, signing serialized data, implementing robust input validation, and isolating deserialization environments. Always be vigilant and audit your code for potential deserialization vulnerabilities. By understanding these risks and adopting secure handling strategies, we can prevent attackers from turning our object handling mechanisms into pathways for attack. In the next chapter, we'll focus on the risks associated with using components with known vulnerabilities.

Chapter 12:

Using Components with Known Vulnerabilities: Managing Your Dependencies.

In today's development landscape, we rarely build everything from scratch. We rely heavily on third-party libraries, frameworks, and other software components to speed up development and leverage existing functionality. However, these components can also introduce security risks if they contain known vulnerabilities that are not properly managed.

Think of it like building a house with pre-fabricated parts. If those parts have structural flaws, your entire house could be compromised. Similarly, if the libraries and frameworks we use in our applications have security weaknesses, our applications become vulnerable to exploitation.

In this chapter, we're going to explore the risks associated with using components with known vulnerabilities, discuss effective dependency management tools and practices, the importance of vulnerability scanning and alerting, strategies for updating and patching dependencies securely, and best practices for choosing and evaluating third-party libraries in the first place.

The Risks of Using Outdated and Vulnerable Libraries: An Open Door for Attackers

Using outdated or vulnerable libraries and frameworks in our web applications poses a significant security risk for several reasons:

- Known Exploits: Once a vulnerability is discovered in a popular component, attackers often develop exploits to target applications using that vulnerable version. These exploits can be readily available, making it easy for even less sophisticated attackers to compromise our systems.

- Increased Attack Surface: Every third-party component we include in our application adds to its overall attack surface. If these components are not well-maintained or have security flaws, they become potential entry points for attackers.
- Chain Reactions: A vulnerability in a seemingly minor dependency can sometimes be exploited to compromise more critical parts of our application or even the underlying system.
- Compliance Issues: Many security standards and regulations require organizations to keep their software up-to-date and address known vulnerabilities. Using outdated components can lead to compliance violations and penalties.

Dependency Management Tools and Practices (e.g., npm, Maven, pip): Keeping Track of Your Building Blocks

The first step in managing the security of our dependencies is to have a clear understanding of what those dependencies are. This is where dependency management tools come in handy.

These tools help us:

- Declare Dependencies: Define the third-party libraries and frameworks our project relies on.
- Manage Versions: Specify the versions of these components we are using.
- Resolve Transitive Dependencies: Handle the dependencies of our direct dependencies.
- Build Reproducible Builds: Ensure that we are using consistent versions of our dependencies across different environments.

Common dependency management tools include:

npm (Node Package Manager) for JavaScript: Manages packages for Node.js projects. Uses a package.json file to define dependencies.

Maven for Java: A powerful build automation tool that also manages dependencies using a pom.xml file.

pip (Package Installer for Python) for Python: Installs and manages packages from the Python Package Index (PyPI). Uses a requirements.txt file (or more modern approaches like pyproject.toml with Poetry or PDM).

Bundler for Ruby: Manages gem dependencies for Ruby projects using a Gemfile.

Composer for PHP: Manages dependencies for PHP projects using a composer.json file.

Best Practices for Dependency Management:

Explicitly Declare Dependencies: Clearly list all the third-party components your application uses in your project's dependency manifest file.

Pin Versions (or Use Version Ranges Carefully): While using the latest version might seem ideal, it can sometimes introduce breaking changes. Consider pinning to specific stable versions or using version ranges with caution to allow for minor and patch updates while avoiding major version upgrades without testing.

Regularly Review Your Dependencies: Periodically review your list of dependencies to ensure you still need them and that they are actively maintained.

Use a Package Lock File: Tools like package-lock.json (npm), pom.xml.lock (Maven with a plugin), pip.lock (Poetry/PDM), and Gemfile.lock (Bundler) ensure that you are using the exact same versions of all direct and transitive dependencies across your development, testing, and production environments. Commit these lock files to your version control system.

Vulnerability Scanning and Alerting: Finding the Cracks in Your Foundation

Just knowing our dependencies isn't enough; we also need to know if any of them have known security vulnerabilities. This is where vulnerability scanning and alerting tools come in. These tools can:

Scan Your Dependencies: Analyze your project's dependency manifest and identify components with publicly disclosed vulnerabilities.

Provide Severity Information: Indicate the severity of the identified vulnerabilities, helping you prioritize remediation efforts.

Offer Remediation Advice: Suggest updated versions or alternative secure components.

Integrate with CI/CD Pipelines: Automate vulnerability scanning as part of your continuous integration and continuous deployment process.

Provide Real-time Alerts: Notify you when new vulnerabilities are discovered in your dependencies.

Popular vulnerability scanning and alerting tools include:

OWASP Dependency-Check: A free and open-source tool that identifies known vulnerabilities in project dependencies.

Snyk: A commercial tool with a free tier that provides vulnerability scanning, automated fixes, and integration with various development workflows.

WhiteSource (now Mend): A commercial platform for software composition analysis, including vulnerability management.

npm audit (for Node.js): A built-in command in npm that scans your project's dependencies for vulnerabilities.

pip check (for Python): A built-in command in pip that verifies installed packages against PyPI's advisory database.

GitHub Security Alerts: GitHub can automatically detect vulnerable dependencies in your repositories and alert you.

Strategies for Updating and Patching Dependencies Securely: Fixing the Flaws

Once vulnerabilities are identified, it's crucial to have a plan for updating and patching the affected dependencies securely:

Prioritize Vulnerabilities: Focus on addressing high-severity vulnerabilities first, especially those with known exploits.

Test Updates Thoroughly: Before deploying updated dependencies to production, thoroughly test them in a staging environment to ensure they don't introduce regressions or break your application.

Follow Release Notes: Review the release notes of the updated components to understand the changes and any potential impact on your application.

Consider Minor and Patch Updates First: When possible, start by updating to minor or patch versions, as these are less likely to introduce breaking changes than major version upgrades.

Major Version Upgrades Require More Care: Major version upgrades often include significant changes and might require code modifications in your application. Plan these upgrades carefully and allocate sufficient time for testing.

Automated Updates (with Caution and Monitoring): Some tools offer automated updates. If you use them, ensure you have robust monitoring and rollback mechanisms in place.

Communicate Updates: Inform your team about dependency updates, especially if they require code changes.

Best Practices for Choosing and Evaluating Third-Party Libraries: Building on a Solid Foundation

The security of our applications starts with the choices we make about the components we include. Here are some best practices for selecting and evaluating third-party libraries:

Reputation and Trustworthiness: Choose libraries that are well-established, actively maintained, and have a good reputation in the community. Look for projects with a significant number of contributors and a history of regular updates and security fixes.

Security Record: Research the library's security history. Have there been past vulnerabilities? How were they addressed? Does the project have a clear security policy?

Maintenance and Activity: Check how active the project is. Are there regular commits? Are issues and pull requests being addressed in a timely manner? An abandoned or poorly maintained library is a security risk.

License: Understand the license of the library and ensure it's compatible with your project's licensing requirements.

Code Quality and Reviews: If possible, review the library's code for security best practices and potential vulnerabilities. Look for projects that undergo security reviews.

Minimize Dependencies: Only include libraries that provide essential functionality. Avoid adding unnecessary dependencies, as each one increases your attack surface.

Consider Alternatives: If a popular library has a history of security issues or is no longer actively maintained, explore secure and well-maintained alternatives.

In Conclusion:

Managing dependencies with known vulnerabilities is a critical aspect of web application security that we, as developers, cannot afford to ignore. By using dependency management tools effectively, implementing regular vulnerability scanning and alerting, following secure update practices, and being diligent in our selection and evaluation of third-party libraries, we can significantly reduce the risk of our applications being compromised through vulnerable components. Staying proactive in this area is essential for building and maintaining secure and resilient web applications. In the next chapter, we'll discuss another crucial security practice: Insufficient Logging and Monitoring.

Chapter 13:

Insufficient Logging and Monitoring: The Eyes and Ears of Your Security Posture.

Think of logging and monitoring as the security cameras and alarm systems for your web application and infrastructure. If you don't have proper logging in place, you won't have a record of what happened during a security incident, making it incredibly difficult to understand the attack, identify the scope of the compromise, and take effective remediation steps. Similarly, without adequate monitoring and alerting, you might not even realize you're under attack until significant damage has already been done.

In this chapter, we're going to explore the importance of comprehensive logging for security, what kind of information we should be logging and how, secure logging practices to prevent information leaks, the necessity of implementing effective monitoring and alerting systems, and the crucial role developers play in incident response.

The Importance of Comprehensive Logging for Security: Recording the Story
Comprehensive logging provides an invaluable record of events that occur within our web applications and their underlying infrastructure. This information is crucial for several security-related reasons:

- Incident Response: When a security incident occurs, logs are essential for understanding the attacker's actions, identifying compromised systems or data, and determining the root cause of the breach. Without detailed logs, incident response becomes a much more difficult and time-consuming process.

- Forensic Analysis: Logs can provide the necessary evidence for forensic analysis after a security incident, helping to reconstruct the timeline of events and potentially identify the attackers.

- Security Monitoring and Threat Detection: By analyzing log data, we can identify suspicious patterns, unusual activity, or potential attacks in progress. This allows for proactive threat detection and timely intervention.

- Compliance and Auditing: Many security standards and regulations require organizations to maintain detailed logs for auditing purposes and to demonstrate compliance.

- Debugging and Troubleshooting: While primarily for development, logs can also help identify and troubleshoot security-related issues or misconfigurations.

What Information Should Be Logged and How? The Details That Matter

Determining what information to log and how to log it effectively is critical. We need to capture enough detail to be useful for security purposes without overwhelming our logging systems or inadvertently logging sensitive data in a way that creates new risks. Here are some key types of information we should consider logging:

- Authentication and Authorization Events: Successful and failed login attempts, account lockouts, password resets, changes to user roles or permissions, and access to protected resources.

- Input Validation Failures: Instances where user input is rejected due to validation rules. This can indicate potential probing by attackers.

- Application Errors and Exceptions: Errors that occur within the application, especially those related to security functions or handling of user input.
- Access to Sensitive Data: Records of when sensitive data is accessed, by whom, and from where.

- Security-Related Configuration Changes: Modifications to security settings, such as firewall rules, access control lists, or encryption keys.

- System Events: Operating system and server-level events that might be relevant to security, such as system reboots, service restarts, or user account changes.

- Network Activity: Logs of network connections, especially those originating from or destined for suspicious IP addresses.

- Web Server Access Logs: Records of all HTTP requests to the web server, including timestamps, source IPs, requested URLs, user agents, and response codes.

How to Log Effectively:

- Timestamps: Ensure all log entries include accurate timestamps.
- Source Information: Record the source of the event (e.g., user ID, IP address, application component).
- Severity Levels: Use log levels (e.g., DEBUG, INFO, WARNING, ERROR, CRITICAL) to indicate the importance of the event.
- Structured Logging: Use a structured logging format (like JSON) to make logs easier to parse, search, and analyze.
- Centralized Logging: Aggregate logs from all components of your application and infrastructure into a centralized logging system. This simplifies analysis and correlation of events.

Secure Logging Practices: Preventing Information Leaks in Your Records

While logging is crucial for security, we also need to be careful not to inadvertently log sensitive information in a way that could create new vulnerabilities. Here are some secure logging practices:

- Avoid Logging Sensitive Data: Do not log sensitive data like passwords (even hashed), API keys, credit card numbers, or other confidential information directly in your application logs. If you need to log information related to these, consider logging only a non-sensitive identifier or a masked version.

- Secure Log Storage: Store logs in a secure location with appropriate access controls. Restrict access to log files and logging systems to authorized personnel only.

- Protect Log Integrity: Implement measures to prevent unauthorized modification or deletion of log data. Consider using log signing or other integrity protection mechanisms.

- Regularly Review Log Retention Policies: Establish and adhere to log retention policies that balance security needs with storage limitations and compliance requirements.
- Secure Transmission of Logs: If you are transmitting logs to a centralized logging system over a network, ensure that the transmission is encrypted (e.g., using TLS).

Implementing Effective Monitoring and Alerting Systems: Proactive Defense

Logging provides the record of events, but monitoring involves actively watching those logs and other system metrics for signs of suspicious activity or potential security incidents. Alerting involves setting up notifications to be triggered when certain thresholds or patterns are detected. Effective monitoring and alerting allow for proactive defense and timely response.

What to Monitor:

Authentication Failures: A high number of failed login attempts from a single IP address could indicate a brute-force attack.

Access to Restricted Resources: Attempts to access sensitive files or administrative interfaces by unauthorized users.

Unusual Traffic Patterns: Significant spikes or drops in network traffic, or traffic from unusual geographic locations.

Error Rates: Sudden increases in application error rates or specific security-related errors.

System Resource Usage: Abnormal CPU or memory usage that could indicate a denial-of-service attack or malware activity.

Security Tool Alerts: Output from intrusion detection systems (IDS), web application firewalls (WAFs), and other security tools.

Changes to Critical Configurations: Unauthorized modifications to system or application configurations.

Implementing Monitoring and Alerting:

Choose Appropriate Tools: Utilize security information and event management (SIEM) systems, log analysis tools, and infrastructure monitoring platforms to collect, analyze, and visualize log data and system metrics.

Define Clear Alerting Rules: Establish specific rules and thresholds that trigger alerts when suspicious activity is detected. Fine-tune these rules to minimize false positives.

Prioritize Alerts: Categorize alerts based on severity and ensure that critical alerts are responded to promptly.

Integrate with Incident Response Processes: Ensure that security alerts are integrated into your incident response workflows.

Developer's Role in Incident Response: Being Part of the Solution

When a security incident occurs, developers play a crucial role in the response process. Their understanding of the application's code, architecture, and logs is invaluable for:

Analyzing Logs: Developers can help security teams understand application-specific logs and identify patterns related to the incident.

Identifying Vulnerabilities: They can assist in pinpointing the vulnerabilities that were exploited.

Developing Fixes: Developers are responsible for developing and deploying patches to address the identified vulnerabilities.

Rebuilding and Recovering Systems: They may be involved in rebuilding compromised systems or recovering data.

Improving Security Measures: Developers can contribute to improving the application's security posture based on the lessons learned from the incident.

In Conclusion:

Insufficient logging and monitoring can leave our web applications operating in the dark, making it easy for attackers to go undetected and difficult to respond effectively when incidents occur. By implementing comprehensive and secure logging practices, establishing robust monitoring and alerting systems, and ensuring developers are an integral part of the incident response process, we can significantly enhance our ability to detect, understand, and mitigate security threats. These practices are not just about compliance; they are about providing the visibility we need to protect our applications and our users. In the next part of the book, we'll shift our focus to mastering HTTP Security Headers for robust protection.

Part 3:

Mastering HTTP Security Headers for Robust Protection

Chapter 14:

HTTP Security Headers: Your First Line of Defense.

We've talked a lot about server-side and client-side vulnerabilities, but HTTP security headers provide a powerful and relatively straightforward way to enhance the security of our web applications by instructing the browser on how to behave.

Think of HTTP security headers as the instructions you give to a visitor entering your house. You can tell them to only use certain doors, to avoid certain rooms, and to be careful about what they bring inside. Similarly, HTTP security headers tell the browser how to handle your website's resources, reducing the risk of various attacks.

In this chapter, we're going to explore the most important HTTP security headers, how they work, and how to implement them effectively to protect our users from attacks like XSS, clickjacking, and more.

What are HTTP Security Headers? Controlling Browser Behavior

HTTP security headers are response headers that we, as developers, send from our web servers to the browser. These headers provide instructions to the browser on how to handle the website's resources and content. They are a crucial part of a defense-in-depth strategy, providing an extra layer of security beyond our application's code.

Key Benefits of Using HTTP Security Headers:

- Mitigate Common Attacks: They help prevent various attacks, including Cross-Site Scripting (XSS), Clickjacking, and MIME-sniffing vulnerabilities.
- Enforce Security Policies: They allow us to enforce security policies at the browser level, limiting the browser's capabilities to reduce the attack surface.

- Improve User Security: By instructing the browser to behave in a secure manner, we can protect our users from various client-side threats.
- Relatively Easy to Implement: Implementing HTTP security headers is often a matter of configuring our web server or application framework.

Essential HTTP Security Headers:
- Content Security Policy (CSP): The most powerful and versatile HTTP security header. CSP allows us to define a whitelist of trusted sources for various types of resources (scripts, styles, images, fonts, etc.). The browser will block any resources that violate this policy. CSP is the primary defense against XSS attacks.
  Example:
  Content-Security-Policy: default-src 'self'; script-src 'self' https://trusted-cdn.com; style-src 'self' 'unsafe-inline'; img-src *

- HTTP Strict Transport Security (HSTS): Enforces the use of HTTPS (secure HTTP) for communication. When a browser receives this header, it will automatically convert any HTTP links to HTTPS and refuse to connect if a valid HTTPS connection cannot be established. This protects against man-in-the-middle attacks and protocol downgrade attacks.

Example:
Strict-Transport-Security: max-age=31536000; includeSubDomains; preload

- X-Frame-Options: Prevents clickjacking attacks by controlling whether a website can be embedded in a <frame>, <iframe>, or <object>.
- Values: DENY (prevents any framing), SAMEORIGIN (allows framing only from the same origin), ALLOW-FROM uri (allows framing from a specific URI).
  Example: X-Frame-Options: SAMEORIGIN

- X-Content-Type-Options: Prevents MIME-sniffing vulnerabilities. When set to nosniff, it instructs the browser to strictly follow the MIME types specified in the Content-Type header and not try to guess the content type. This can prevent attackers from uploading malicious files disguised as harmless ones.

Example:

X-Content-Type-Options: nosniff

- X-XSS-Protection: This header was designed to prevent XSS attacks in older browsers. However, it can sometimes introduce vulnerabilities and is largely superseded by CSP. It's generally recommended not to use this header or to explicitly disable it.

Example (to disable):

X-XSS-Protection: 0

- Referrer-Policy: Controls how much referrer information (the URL of the previous page) is sent with requests. This can help protect user privacy and prevent information leakage.

Example:

Referrer-Policy: strict-origin-when-cross-origin

- Permissions-Policy (formerly Feature-Policy): Allows you to control which web platform features (like geolocation, microphone, camera) are available to your website. This can help reduce the attack surface and prevent malicious use of these features.

Example:

Permissions-Policy: geolocation=() (disables geolocation)

Implementing HTTP Security Headers:

HTTP security headers are typically implemented at the web server level (e.g., Apache, Nginx) or within your application framework. The specific configuration methods will vary depending on your setup.

- Web Server Configuration: Most web servers allow you to set headers in their configuration files (e.g., .htaccess for Apache, nginx.conf for Nginx).

- Application Frameworks: Many web frameworks provide mechanisms for setting HTTP headers in your application code.
- Middleware: You can also use middleware components in your application to set HTTP security headers.

Testing and Validating HTTP Security Headers:
It's crucial to test and validate your HTTP security header configuration to ensure they are working correctly and not causing any unexpected issues.

- Browser Developer Tools: Use your browser's developer tools to inspect the HTTP response headers and verify that the security headers are being sent with the correct values.
- Online Tools: There are online tools (like securityheaders.com) that can analyze your website's HTTP headers and provide recommendations.

Best Practices for Using HTTP Security Headers:

- Start with a Strong CSP: Content Security Policy is the most important security header. Start by defining a strict CSP that allows only necessary resources and gradually loosen it as needed, monitoring for any violations.
- Use HTTPS and HSTS: Always use HTTPS for your website and implement HSTS to enforce secure connections.
- Test Thoroughly: Test your HTTP security header configuration in a staging environment before deploying to production.
- Monitor for Issues: Monitor your application for any issues caused by your HTTP security header configuration. CSP violations, in particular, should be monitored closely.
- Keep Up-to-Date: Stay informed about new HTTP security headers and best practices.

HTTP Security Headers are a Powerful Tool

HTTP security headers are a powerful and relatively easy-to-implement tool for enhancing the security of our web applications. By understanding these headers and implementing them effectively, we can provide a crucial layer of defense against a wide range of attacks and protect our users from client-side threats. In the next chapter, we'll shift our focus to server-side request forgery (SSRF) and how to protect our applications from attacks that abuse server-side requests.

Chapter 15:

Advanced Security Topics and the Future of Web Security.

Throughout this book, we've built a solid foundation in web application security, covering the OWASP Top Ten and the crucial role of HTTP Security Headers. But the world of cybersecurity is constantly evolving, with new threats emerging and new defense mechanisms being developed.

In this concluding chapter, we're going to broaden our horizons and touch upon some more advanced security topics that are increasingly relevant in modern web development. We'll explore the role of Web Application Firewalls (WAFs), strategies for Rate Limiting and protecting against DDoS attacks, the unique security challenges in microservices and API architectures, some of the emerging trends and technologies in web security, and finally, the absolute necessity of continuous learning for us as developers in this ever-changing landscape.

Web Application Firewalls (WAFs) and Their Role in Defense: The Gatekeepers at the Application Level

We've talked about network firewalls that protect our infrastructure at the network level. Web Application Firewalls (WAFs) operate at a higher level, specifically designed to protect web applications from HTTP-based attacks. Think of a WAF as a security guard that sits between your web application and the internet, inspecting incoming HTTP requests and filtering out malicious ones before they even reach your application code.

How WAFs Work:

WAFs typically use a set of rules or signatures to identify and block common web application attacks, such as:
 * SQL Injection (SQLi)
 * Cross-Site Scripting (XSS)
 * Cross-Site Request Forgery (CSRF)
 * Directory Traversal
 * File Inclusion Attacks
 * Denial of Service (DoS) attempts

WAFs can be implemented in various ways:
- Hardware-based appliances: Dedicated hardware devices that sit in your network.
- Software-based solutions: Software that runs on your servers.
- Cloud-based services: Managed security services offered by cloud providers or specialized security vendors.

Benefits of Using a WAF:
- Protection Against Known Attacks: WAFs are regularly updated with rules to block the latest known attack patterns.

- Virtual Patching: WAFs can provide a form of "virtual patching" by blocking exploits against known vulnerabilities in your application or its components, even before you have a chance to apply a code-level patch.
- Customizable Rules: WAFs can be configured with custom rules tailored to your specific application's needs and potential threats.
- Centralized Security Management: Cloud-based WAFs often provide a centralized platform for managing security policies across multiple web applications.
- Logging and Reporting: WAFs provide detailed logs of blocked requests and attack attempts, which can be valuable for security analysis and incident response.

Important Considerations for WAFs:
- Not a Silver Bullet: A WAF is a valuable layer of defense but should not be considered a replacement for secure coding practices. Vulnerabilities in your

application code can still be exploited if not properly addressed.

- Configuration is Key: An improperly configured WAF can block legitimate traffic or fail to block malicious requests. Careful tuning and maintenance are essential.
- False Positives: WAFs can sometimes block legitimate requests (false positives). It's important to monitor for these and adjust the rules accordingly.

Rate Limiting and DDoS Protection for Web Applications: Staying Online Under Attack

Rate limiting is a security mechanism that restricts the number of requests a user or IP address can make to your web application within a specific time window. This helps to prevent brute-force attacks (like password guessing) and can also mitigate some forms of Denial of Service (DoS) attacks.

Denial of Service (DoS) and Distributed Denial of Service (DDoS) attacks aim to overwhelm your web application and its infrastructure with a flood of malicious traffic, making it unavailable to legitimate users. DDoS attacks involve using a distributed network of compromised computers (a botnet) to amplify the attack volume.

Strategies for Rate Limiting:
- Implement at the Application Level: Many web frameworks offer built-in rate limiting middleware or libraries.
- Use Web Server Modules: Web servers like Nginx and Apache have modules for rate limiting.
- Cloud-Based Services: Cloud providers and CDN (Content Delivery Network) services often offer robust rate limiting capabilities.

Strategies for DDoS Protection:
- Over-Provisioning Bandwidth: Having more bandwidth than usual traffic can help absorb smaller DDoS attacks.
- Content Delivery Networks (CDNs): CDNs can distribute your website's content across multiple servers globally,

making it harder for attackers to overwhelm a single point. They often have built-in DDoS mitigation features.

- DDoS Mitigation Services: Specialized cloud-based services offer advanced DDoS protection, including traffic scrubbing, filtering, and absorbing large-scale attacks.
- Traffic Analysis and Filtering: Implementing systems to analyze incoming traffic and filter out malicious requests based on patterns, source IPs, and other characteristics.
- Infrastructure Design: Designing your infrastructure to be resilient to high traffic loads and having redundancy in place.

Security in Microservices and API Architectures: Distributed Security Challenges

Modern web applications are increasingly built using microservices – small, independent services that communicate with each other over

APIs. This distributed architecture introduces new security challenges:

API Security: Securing the APIs that connect microservices is crucial. This includes authentication, authorization, input validation, and protection against API-specific attacks.

Service-to-Service Authentication and Authorization: Ensuring that only authorized services can communicate with each other. Techniques like mutual TLS (mTLS) and secure tokens are often used.

Distributed Tracing and Logging: Tracking requests and security events across multiple services can be complex but is essential for debugging and security analysis.

Configuration Management: Securely managing configurations and secrets across a distributed environment.

Network Segmentation: Isolating microservices within the network to limit the impact of a compromise in one service.

Service Mesh Security: Using a service mesh to provide features like secure communication, traffic management, and observability across services.

Emerging Web Security Trends and Technologies: Staying Ahead of the Curve

The field of web security is constantly evolving. As developers, we need to be aware of emerging trends and technologies to stay ahead of potential threats:

- Zero Trust Security: A security model based on the principle of "never trust, always verify." This involves strict identity verification for every user and device trying to access resources, regardless of their location.
- Security Automation (DevSecOps): Integrating security practices and tools into the software development lifecycle (SDLC) to automate security testing, vulnerability scanning, and compliance checks.
- AI and Machine Learning for Security: Using AI and ML to analyze security data,

detect anomalies, and predict potential threats.

- Privacy-Enhancing Technologies (PETs): Technologies that allow data to be processed or analyzed while preserving privacy, such as homomorphic encryption and differential privacy.
- WebAssembly (Wasm) for Security: Exploring the potential of Wasm to run code in a sandboxed environment in the browser or on the server, potentially enhancing security for certain types of applications.
- Decentralized Web (Web3) Security: Understanding the unique security challenges and opportunities in decentralized applications built on blockchain technologies.

Continuous Learning and Staying Updated in the Cybersecurity Landscape for Developers: A Lifelong Journey

Finally, and perhaps most importantly, cybersecurity is not a destination but a continuous journey. The threat landscape is constantly changing, new vulnerabilities are discovered, and new attack techniques emerge. For us as developers, continuous learning is absolutely essential to stay informed and effective in building secure web applications.

How to Stay Updated:

- Follow Security Blogs and News: Stay informed about the latest security news, trends, and vulnerabilities.
- Read Security Research Papers and Reports: Delve deeper into specific security topics and research findings.
- Attend Security Conferences and Webinars: Learn from experts and network with other security professionals.
- Participate in Security Communities: Engage in online forums, mailing lists, and social media groups focused on web security.
- Take Security Training and Courses: Invest in formal security training to deepen your knowledge and skills.

- Experiment with Security Tools: Get hands-on experience with security scanning tools, WAFs, and other security technologies.
- Follow OWASP and Other Security Organizations: Stay updated on their latest projects, guidelines, and best practices.

Your Role as a Security-Conscious Developer: As developers, we are on the front lines of web security. By embracing a security-first mindset, understanding common vulnerabilities, implementing secure coding practices, and staying informed about the evolving threat landscape, we can play a crucial role in building a more secure web for everyone.

This book has provided you with a strong foundation in OWASP essentials and HTTP security headers. But remember, this is just the beginning. Continue to learn, continue to practice, and continue to make security a priority in everything you build. The security of our digital world depends on it.